BEYOND THE HIDDEN PAIN OF Abortion

PATRICIA A. BIGLIARDI

Women's Aglow Fellowship International
P.O. Box 1548
Lynnwood, WA 98046-1548
USA

Cover design by David Marty

Women's Aglow Fellowship International is an interdenominational organization of Christian women. Our mission is to lead women to Jesus Christ and provide opporunity for Christian women to grow in their faith and minister to others.

Our publications are used to help women find a personal relationship with Jesus Christ, to enhance growth in their Christian experience, and to help them recognize their roles and relationship according to Scripture.

For more information about Women's Aglow Fellowship, please write to Women's Aglow Fellowship International, P.O. Box 1548, Lynnwood, WA 98046-1548, USA or call (206) 775-7282.

Unless otherwise noted, all scripture quotations in this publication are from the Holy Bible, New King James Version. Copyright © 1979, 1980, 1982, Thomas Nelson, Inc. Other versions are abbreviated as follows: KJV (King James Version), NAS (New American Standard), NIV (New International Version), TAB (The Amplified Bible), TLB (The Living Bible).

ISBN 1-56616-011-1

1 2 3 4 Printing / Year 97 96 95 94

Dedication

I wish to dedicate this book to the children
of the next generation:

to
Heather Marie Stamps
and
Donald Austin Hejny
who both pray daily that the lives of all unborn babies
will be spared from abortion. Thank you for teaching me
the power of a child's prayer.

to
Matthew Nicholas Lynam
who has always ministered the love of Jesus to me
through his sensitivity and warm hugs.
Thanks for loving me.

And to
Achille (Kelly) Mathew Bigliardi IV,
my son, who had given me a reason to live
my convictions with integrity and compassion,
and who has always brought great joy and laughter
into my life. Thank you for believing in me.
I am your greatest fan, Kelly.

May God bless and keep
this next generation of children.

Acknowledgments

Writing a book can often be a long, lonely path of self-disclosure and self-discipline, but it is never a path taken alone. Many people have contributed their physical, emotional, and spiritual support to this project, so many in fact, that it would be impossible to list them all here. To a host of friends who have shared their lives with me I owe a great debt of gratitude.

Specifically, I offer my deep appreciate to:

Mary and Sam Loria, my parents, who gave me their love, prayers, and support from my birth until their deaths. Thank you Mom and Dad, you taught me anything was possible with God.

Les Stubbe, who told me this book needed to be written.

Diane Radcliff, who first told me I was a writer and encouraged me to believe in my destiny in God.

Sandra P. Aldrich, my "coach" who said, "Just write the book," when I wanted to give up and go to the beach. Thanks for pushing me toward the finishing line.

Gail and Vic Chernoff: From the day we sat at your kitchen table until today you believed in me and this book. Your support and faith never waned. You are special friends; thank you for making me a part of your family.

Karen E. Anderson, my editor, whose loving feedback and words of encouragement turned a working relationshp into an eternal friendship, my deepest gratitude to you.

Women's Aglow Fellowship International, thank you for the privilege of working with all of you. It has been one of the greatest experiences of my life. Your prayers and faith in a rookie author were astounding.

Face to Face Ministry supporters, without whose prayers and financial support this book would not have been possible. Thank you, trusting friends.

I also want to honor some people without whom I would not have had the courage to reveal all the truths within this book.

Marietta Stewart, Yvonne Benavidez and Nancy Johnson, who prayed daily for me and this book for over four years.

Patricia Aizawa and Joyce Woodman, who listened patiently while I shared my pain and held me in their prayers throughout this project.

Pastor Mike Woodman and Trinity Foursquare Church in San Jose, California, thanks for ministering to me and bringing me closer to Jesus.

Janice Morris, who has held me and wiped away my tears in my darkest hours, thank you for your soft entreaties on my behalf.

And to a very special group of people, the women who have shared their stories in this book, thank you for your courage and confidence. Some of the names and details of their lives have been changed to protect their privacy.

Most of all, to my family: Thank you Mary, Craig, Heather, Rachael, Sara, Kevin, and Joshua Stamps, Lorraine and Melinda Loria, and Kelly Bigliardi for loving me through until the end. Your personal sacrifice was deeply appreciated. And yes, Kelly, I wrote the book!

Pat Bigliardi
San Jose, California
August, 1994

Contents

1
...
The Decision

I took a deep breath, braced myself, and pressed the familiar numbers on the dial. The phone rang as I paced back and forth, stretching my neck to the right and to the left, raising my shoulders in an attempt to relax my body like a runner before an important race.

"IDT."

I felt my heart racing, a slight tremor pulsed through me.

"Is Kelly available?"

The click at the other end of the line told me I was being connected. *What is he going to say when he hears the news?* My eyes quickly scanned the picture in the gold frame next to the phone. It was my favorite. The tall, good looking young man with broad shoulders stood ramrod straight, proudly holding a small boy who sat relaxed and

trusting in his father's arms. Both had warm brown eyes and wide grins that arrested attention and sent a smile racing across my face. Kelly and little Kelly. These were the men in my life and I loved them deeply.

"Kelly here." The voice was etched in stress.

"Hi, honey, how's your day going?" I tried to sound soothing.

"I've been in meetings all morning, and I have another one scheduled in just a few minutes, so I don't have long to talk. What's up?"

I looked around the room for assurance: neutral toned grasscloth covered the walls, and custom made over-stuffed furniture projected just the right air of casual elegance I desired. It was right in style with California's affluence in the '70s.

"I just got back from an appointment with Dr. Halliday." I paused to form exactly the right phrasing. "I have some good news and some bad news." I hoped humor would soften the unexpected.

"Give me the good news. I need to hear some good news today."

I laughed nervously. "You're not sterile."

Silence rose out of the phone toward me like thick smoke. Then I heard a taut exhale.

"Are you serious? You're kidding, right?" His voice strained the words out as my eyes darted to the expansive windows. "This is probably the worst time for us to have to deal with a new baby." The irritation in his voice was unmistakable. "I can't believe it. How could this have happened?"

Suddenly the smile I'd had all morning vanished.

Kelly lowered his voice but there was no warmth in it. "Pat, I don't want another baby." The finality of his words lay between us like a gravestone. "Listen, I'll support

your decision either way, but I want you to know *I don't want this baby.*"

My mind raced on. *He decided just like that . . . "I don't want this baby."* It held onto a flicker of inconsistency: *so what does it mean that he'll support my decision either way?* My knees folded beneath me and I slumped down on the couch. *He said it so easily.*

Eight years before, Kelly found an unexpected greeting waiting for him on his dinner plate: Welcome Home, Daddy! A shy grin skidded across his face until it burst into a dazzled smile of pure delight.

Now, staring absently at the phone, I hardly recognized my own voice. "I wouldn't want to bring a baby into this world without the same excitement that greeted Little Kelly. Every child deserves to be wanted." My hollow litany echoed with such emptiness that I squared my shoulders, sat up straight, and forced my voice to take on a tone of intellectual rationality. I wasn't going to allow myself to expose my need for his support.

"I'll make an appointment with Dr. Poppy," I said matter-of-factly. "I'll discuss the various options with him."

"That's a good idea," he answered too quickly. He was silent again before the conversation ended with, "I can't believe you've let this happen." I could hear his other line ringing in the background. "We'll discuss it later, when I get home." Abruptly he hung up the phone.

Slowly, I placed the receiver down.

My eyes moved back to father and son in the gold picture frame as sadness flooded over me. Our marriage had been turbulent, scarred by disillusionment and even betrayal, but our love for each other had held us together through two separations. Surely another child could only help heal the wounds and make us a family again.

I didn't move from the couch. *Has it been only five*

months since we moved here? I had grown comfortable and secure for the first time in our marriage. After 12 years together, we were putting down roots, becoming part of a community.

Our new townhome represented the dreams I had dared to dream but thought were dashed when he filed for divorce two years before.

Instead, we were starting over. "Dreams do come true," I told our friends.

The drive home from the doctor's office earlier that morning had been filled with such expectation. Weaving through the soft undulating foothills that escort Highway 280 from Los Altos to San Jose, I had allowed my happiness to bubble to the surface. A baby. How I'd longed to have another child: to feel the warmth of its body as I held it close, to watch its small mouth sucking at my breast, to smell the sweetness of mother's milk on its breath. I wanted to shout to the world, "I'm pregnant!" Emotions ran together: elation, joy, jubilation, wonder. A new life had begun to form in me.

Didn't Kelly know how much I'd wanted another baby? Struggling to maintain control, I didn't want to acknowledge—even to myself—the anger welling up inside me.

But how could he know? I had hidden my desire from him. Not wanting to pressure him, I waited to discuss the possibility of another child when our lives were more settled. Now, by some turn of fate my plan had been taken out of my hands. *Couldn't he at least be curious about my dreams?*

Why didn't he ask, "How do you feel about this? What do you want, Pat"? My shock at his reaction was wearing off. In its place I felt the sharp sting of his rejection. At that moment, without my knowing it, a steel door slammed shut deep inside of me.

12

The Decision

Two days later I drove down the familiar winding, oak and pine studded street and remembered the warm, cared-for feelings of eight years ago. The same routed wood sign, hanging from two linked chains, squeaked back and forth at me as I pulled into the parking lot. Los Altos Medical Clinic, it announced, Dr. Poppy, Dr. Murphy, Dr. Mcguire.

The long, ranch-style brick gynecology clinic with its heavy shake roof looked undisturbed by time.

Peering through the beveled glass window, I opened the heavy oak door and was surprised. Except for new paint and reupholstered benches, the round waiting room with its twisted old oak tree in the center atrium looked the same. I had always loved coming here. Now its familiarity brought a sense of nostalgia for the time when each visit brought me closer to the birth of my first child, when our lives were fresh and exciting.

I glanced around at the other women waiting patiently to be seen, each at a different stage of pregnancy. Some looked uncomfortable and irritable. Others reminded me of myself as a first-time mother-to-be, filled with hope, yet anxiously awaiting the unknown.

Today I felt awkward and out-of-place; I was grateful no one suspected the real reason I was there.

As I sat down on a padded bench, as memories of my first pregnancy washed over my thoughts. After each doctor's visit I'd hurry home. There in the quiet solitude of our small apartment, I'd lie on the couch and study the prenatal book with its amazing photographs. I'd diligently read each caption in search of the one that described my baby's stage of development.

Hey little one, you don't look like a toad anymore. . . . Ten weeks, wow, you have fingers and toes now. . . . The doctor said he could hear your heart beat today. . . . Are

13

you a boy or a girl? . . . Will I know how to take care of you? . . . Will you look like me or your daddy? . . . What will you be like when you're grown? I wondered if my baby knew my thoughts.

The first time I felt life stir within me, it was such a small flutter, I almost missed it. *What was that? There it was again. Is it what I think? Yes! It's the baby, it's moving. I felt it!* With each passing month the movements became more noticeable: twisting, tumbling, then a strong flutter-kick here and a thrusting fist there. At nine months I could feel his whole body shifting from one side to another.

I was enthralled by the miracle of it all. Now, I longed to feel, once again, the unique sensation of movement stirring inside of me, movement I had no control over, sensations separate and apart from my own.

"Mrs. Bigliardi?" The nurse's voice drew me back to the present.

After taking my temperature and blood pressure she led me into a large sunlit room. Its walls were lined floor-to-ceiling with bookshelves and an impressive array of formal degrees and association memberships. A massive cherry-wood desk, polished to a rich luster, dominated the center of the room.

"Well, Pat, it's been a long time since I last saw you," Dr. Poppy said cheerfully before closing the door behind him. As he strode to his big, burgundy leather, wingback chair I realized I had forgotten how imposing a six-foot-seven inch doctor can be.

Except for slightly graying hair, his handsome, athletic good looks were the same. Only his white lab coat pocket stuffed with stethoscope, pens, and prescription pads gave notice of his profession. Underneath, he lived in uncreased pants and loafers. He folded down into his chair like a long-legged flamingo and leaned back before looking at me.

14

"So, Pat how have you been?"

"Pretty good." I wanted to sound normal. "I'm here because I found out last week from Dr. Halliday, my internist, I'm pregnant." Without meaning to, I leaned forward apprehensively.

"And I'm concerned about possible complications, considering my age and my medical background."

"Let's see," he said, sitting forward and flipping through my file. "Did you develop toxemia with your first pregnancy? No, you didn't. Good." He looked me in the face. "There's no question, however, we'll have to be careful. I've even managed patients with kidney transplants through successful pregnancies, and I feel confident we can do the same for you," he said, smiling.

Leaning back, he rested his elbows on the arms of the chair. "You may have to spend the last three months in bed, you'll definitely have to get your weight down, and I'll have to cautiously monitor your blood pressure."

I looked down. "Doctor, there is one more thing," I hesitated. "My marriage is pretty shaky." My throat felt dry. "My husband and I have separated twice since I last saw you. The last time for 15 months. To tell you the truth, I'm not sure if we're going to make it this time."

I paused, my eyes averting his. "What about the possibility of an abortion?" The word slithered out of my mouth.

When I looked up, his facial expression and voice were void of emotional clues. "Well, as you know, it's now legal, and I can't foresee any problems if you're in the first trimester."

"Would there be any emotional ramifications if I chose to have one?" Secretly, I wanted him to answer yes, to give me a reason to reject Kelly's unspoken suggestion.

He paused for a moment, resting his hands on the desk.

"Pat, it's like any other decision. Once you've made it, you'll justify it to yourself." He unfolded deliberately from the chair and moved slowly around the desk. "So, no, I don't think you'll have to worry about any emotional repercussions. Why don't we go ahead and do an exam to see how you're doing?" He opened the door and pointed me toward an examining room.

Changing into the hospital gown, I seized my emotions with my mind: I needed to remain detached, I couldn't allow myself to get too excited until my decision was made.

After the exam, I returned to Dr. Poppy's office. He entered, shut the door behind him, and sat casually across one corner of the desk.

"Pat, everything looks good right now, but if you want to terminate this pregnancy you'll need to make your decision soon." He looked down at me. "I would estimate you're six to seven weeks along." Patting my arm, he smiled. "Why don't you go home and think it over. We'll schedule another appointment in two weeks."

During the half hour drive home my thoughts were like strands of thread weaving together: *six to seven weeks along, he said. They start to look human at that stage. Their eyes are like small buttons, complete with eyelids.* Quickly I suppressed the pictures etched so vividly in my mind eight years ago.

I wanted to be elated, but Kelly's words, "I don't want this baby," played over and over again. Soon a wall of stubborn anger encircled my soul. *He's left me before, he could do it again. Then I'd have two children to raise alone. What choice do I have . . . really have? Face it, Pat, he doesn't want this baby.*

I knew what my decision had to be.

Kelly never brought up the subject, and I didn't bother to discuss what I decided. I would tell Dr. Poppy at my

next scheduled visit. Until then, I pushed it out of my mind. I didn't dare share my secret with anyone.

———————

The following material is for use in support groups or individually.

Abortion is often a symptom of a much deeper pain. Although many of us believe we "chose" to have an abortion, our decision may not have been a fully informed choice. Few, if any of us, were aware of the long-term consequences an abortion experience would have on the rest of our lives. The questions at the end of each chapter are designed to help us gain insight and understanding about the issues which contributed to our abortion experience and to help us deal more effectively with the emotional, physical, and spiritual consequences of abortion.

These initial questions called "Historical Expedition" will help you focus on the possible root causes that led you to seek an abortion and will help lay a foundation of self-awareness as you continue reading.

Historical Expedition
1. At what age did you first become sexually active?

2. Why did you become sexually active?

3. How did you feel after your first sexual experience?

4. Did your feelings of self-worth improve or diminish after your first sexual experience?

5. When did you meet the father of the baby?

6. Did you make a conscious decision to be sexually active in that relationship or did it just happen?

7. What was your understanding of the relationship?

8. What did you tell yourself about the possibility of getting pregnant?

9. Did you and the father discuss the possibility of your becoming pregnant? What was his understanding of what would happen if you became pregnant? What was yours?

10. What do you wish you knew prior to becoming sexually active? Would you have done things differently now than you did then?

INSIGHT QUESTIONS FOR CHAPTER 1

1. Did you tell anyone about the possibility that you might be pregnant? Did they give you any advice?

2. How did you react to their advice?

3. How did you find out you were pregnant? Once yoursuspicians were confirmed, how did you feel?

4. What did you think would happen when you told the father you were pregnant?

5. Did you receive abortion counseling? What were the options presented to you? What was your opinion of abortion before you became pregnant?

6. Did you feel pressured to make the decision you made? Would you make a different decision today? Why or why not?

2

. . .

The Choice
of Grief

"Please, Mommy, please don't kill me. I'm a girl baby just like you. Please don't kill me!" Jolted awake, I shuddered. My racing heartbeat pounded in my head; my breathing rapid and shallow.

I lay still, momentarily held captive by the dark. Gradually, my eyes adjusted to the faint January light filtering through the drapes. The familiar shadows of the trees outside my window reassured me.

Thank God, it was just a dream.

But the memory of the sound of that small voice crying out to me wouldn't go away. Pulling the sheet tighter around me, I huddled closer to my husband. I hoped the warmth of his body would console me, but I lay awake for a long time, frightened, alone. I had no one to confide in.

Beyond the Hidden Pain of Abortion

This decision was mine and mine alone. I only had to hold on a little while longer.

The morning quiet settled in. Kelly left for work, my son was off to school. But the drone of the vacuum cleaner didn't drown out the voice. *"Please, Mommy, don't kill me, I'm a girl baby just like you."*

Finally in anguish I heard myself scream a silent prayer. *Please, God, take this baby. I don't want to kill my baby, but shouldn't it be wanted by both its parents?* I couldn't remember the last time I'd prayed. Would God even hear me?

A few days later I noticed some bleeding. Was I miscarrying naturally? *Oh please, God, let it be so. I don't want to kill my baby. Please take this baby,* I pleaded again.

I locked myself away from Kelly emotionally and never told him about the dream. After all, hadn't he told me what he wanted?

I sat down suddenly. When had we ever really shared intimate parts of ourselves—really talked? That kind of intimacy had never been part of our relationship. Gradually, through our years together, the more unapproachable I sensed he was, the more I talked at him. Finally, like two electrical cords that rub against each other until the wires fray, only sparks flew instead of current.

The spotting continued and I called Dr. Poppy.

"You'd better come in and let me take a look as soon as possible, today." He had a slight urgency in his voice.

When I arrived at his office, I was quickly ushered into an examining room.

I wasn't cold, but I shivered as I lay waiting on the examining table.

"Let's take a look and see what's happening, Pat," Dr. Poppy said as he swept through the door. His face was expressionless, but a tone of concern crept into his voice.

"Pat, your uterus hasn't expanded since your last exam. It should have grown considerably by now. It's probably a good idea if you seriously considered scheduling that D & C. This pregnancy looks like there could be complications."

The surgery was scheduled for Thursday, February 9. As an outpatient, I'd only be in the hospital for a few hours, returning home the same evening.

I awoke apprehensively Thursday morning. The illuminated dial said 6:30 a.m. I stared at the ceiling. *Just walk through it, Pat. It'll be over by the end of the day. Then you'll never have to think about it again.*

I threw back the sheets and forced myself out of bed. Kelly was already awake and in the shower. My inner dialogue with him was biting and sarcastic, but I determined I would remain outwardly pleasant. I was surprised when he volunteered to take time from his pressured schedule, yet he had promised to be supportive, no matter what my decision.

Without thinking, I packed my robe and slippers in a bag, picked up the paper lying on the night stand, and reread the instructions the doctor had given me. "Nothing to eat or drink after midnight." I wasn't looking forward to waking up without coffee.

"How are you doing this morning?" Kelly leaned down to kiss me on the cheek. Wrapped in a towel, his hair still dripping wet from the shower, he looked oblivious to any turmoil I might be experiencing.

"I'm doing okay, I guess."

"I'll get Little Kelly some breakfast. Why don't you take a long hot shower—it's still early."

I turned up the hot water in the shower, letting it pour over my head and neck to try and ease the fatigue I felt. Turning my face toward the spray I wished it could wash

23

away my despondency. This will pass, I thought as twinges of fear crept into my consciousness. Before I knew it, it would be all over. I dressed quickly and went downstairs.

Kelly had gotten our son ready for school, and we planned to drop him off on our way to the hospital. Our seven-year-old was the delight of our lives. Watching his intense and energy-packed body jump from the kitchen chair in his wide wale corduroys and pullover sweater brought a moment of relief to my aching heart.

Absent mindedly, I got out the backgammon set. "I'll bring this along for something to do." I spoke to no one in particular.

We piled into the car, Little Kelly bouncing rambunctiously on the seat in the back, telling what he thought were funny stories. I smiled and nodded as if I were paying attention, but I hadn't heard a word he said.

"Bye, Mom, bye, Dad," he yelled jumping out the door as soon as we pulled up to the school yard. "I'll see you tonight."

"Love you," I called out, but he was already running toward his friends.

Once we pulled away from the school, Kelly and I drove to the hospital in virtual silence. A few trees were beginning to bud on this warm sunny February day. Changing seasons weren't as eventful in California as they had been in Michigan where I grew up. There, after the long frozen months of winter, spring was exciting—its promise of new life invigorating every bare branch and bush. Today, however, I stared out the window numb and distant from the subtle new life emerging around me.

A wide curved boulevard planted with clumps of white-barked birch, eucalyptus, and long-needled pine led us toward the entrance of El Camino Hospital. The five story red brick building with wings on either side was staffed by

some of the most prominent doctors in the Bay Area. Its tastefully decorated lobby quickly informed you that your seclusion would be guarded inside its private domain. As we walked to the information desk I felt self-conscious. "Our patient admissions is to your left," directed the elderly, white haired volunteer dressed in her pink and white striped outfit.

We entered the cubicle where the admitting clerk sat behind her computer ready to ask all the typical questions. But when she inquired, "What type of surgery are you having?" I felt exposed.

"A D & C procedure." I carefully avoided the term therapeutic abortion.

She completed the necessary forms, handed them to me, and told me to follow the blue line on the floor, which would lead me to the special section where all minor surgery was performed.

Dutifully Kelly and I followed the bright blue line down the corridor, through double doors into a second waiting area filled with strangers. Their faces reflected apprehension, concern, and a few, fear. Hospitals had always frightened me; they brought my own mortality too close for me to ignore. I strained to close out sight and sound. I wanted an invisible blanket between me and the rest of the world.

A nurse called my name and led me to my room. As she swept back a privacy curtain, I looked at a beige metal bed, a hospital nightstand and a small chair. At least the blue print bedspreads and drapes were bright and cheery.

Part of me wanted to get this over with but as the nurse moved swiftly and efficiently through her duties, another part felt like screaming, "Please someone stop this, please don't make me do this!" Immediately I pulled out the backgammon set.

At 8:30 promptly, the anesthetist stopped by my room to ready me for surgery. Fast moving and small, he asked me about my medical history in short staccato sentences. When he took my blood pressure, his brows furrowed as he removed his stethoscope and draped it around his neck. He wrote some brief notes on the paper attached to his clipboard before he looked up.

"Mrs. Bigliardi, I'm going to recommend that we postpone your surgery."

"What?" I could feel my body grow tense.

"Your blood pressure is much too high for this type of procedure. I'll inform Dr. Poppy." He turned and left the room abruptly.

I turned my face away. I couldn't will my body not to abort naturally at home. I knew if that happened, I couldn't deal with it. This wasn't going to be some simple little matter. I couldn't bear the thought of waiting one more day.

A few minutes later the phone next to my bed rang.

"Pat, this is Doctor Poppy. The anesthetist won't proceed under these conditions."

"Doctor, please, I just want to get this over with. Can't you use a local anesthetic?"

"Yes, we could, but the anesthetist is afraid complications could develop. He informed me that the slightest deviation in the dosage of anesthesia could cause paralysis."

My mind was so focused on ending this ordeal, even that possibility didn't sink in. "But I don't want to wait. I could hardly handle it today." I heard a child's whine in my voice. "Besides, I'm still spotting and I'm afraid I'll miscarry at home."

"Yes, I know. I'm concerned about that, too. But we'll have to wait until Tuesday. That's the soonest we can reschedule your surgery." His matter-of-fact tone became

soothing, "Try to relax. If you have any problems, call me immediately."

I put the receiver down. "My God, what next?" I muttered through clenched teeth. Kelly looked at me quizzically from his bedside chair.

"My blood pressure is too high today for this type of procedure." Kelly's face revealed an instant of disgust before he forced it back into impassivity.

Monday afternoon arrived after a long tense weekend. I'd been scheduled to check into the hospital the evening before the surgery to give the anesthetist time to examine me thoroughly.

The admitting procedures were the same, but this time I was placed on the gynecology and obstetrics floor. My room had a view of the surrounding foothills, now a deep vibrant green from recent spring rains. Inside, everything was fresh and crisp, the staff warm and friendly.

I was polite to my roommate but not anxious to interact with her on a personal level. A nurse came in to complete the admitting procedure. But she didn't ask me why I was there.

Kelly sat awkwardly, his six-foot-three frame jackknifed into a small chair next to the bed, his arms crossed tightly in front of his chest. I wanted to do anything but lie there and wait.

"Let's go down to the nursery and see the newborn babies," I suggested, slipping on my robe. We walked down the hall arm in arm. Now that I'd accepted that this baby was lost to me, I wanted to be reassured that someday we'd have another child.

Whenever I'd stop by to see a friend in the hospital I'd always sneak up to peer in on the latest arrivals to our world. It never ceased to amaze me—the wonder of life.

Beyond the Hidden Pain of Abortion

How could those little human beings be conceived, survive, and grow inside a women's womb for nine months, then emerge perfect miniature replicas of humanity, special and unique? Each was a brush stroke on the canvas of life: some, like soft pastel watercolors were dabbed delicately on the canvas. Others, like bright, bold oils, were slapped across it with the broad stroke of a palette knife, but each was an original, a personal reflection of a master's hand.

I loved to watch them, their faces scrunched up, diminutive cries coming from minuscule mouths. Jerky arm motions and tiny fists batting at the air shouted their displeasure at being forced into this foreign world.

Parents and relatives, on the other hand, wore wide beaming smiles, made silly facial contortions, and tapped incessantly on the nursery window to get a disinterested baby's attention.

"That's our son, the one with all the black hair?" crowed a young man. "Jason Andrews, Jr.," he continued with a father's pride.

Kelly and I stood aside from the others. We said very little. Even though we turned to look at one other in recognition of some antic we saw, we weren't part of this scene, not this time.

As I stared into the nursery I forced back tears. I tucked my arm in Kelly's again, tried to snuggle close to him, and leaned my head against his shoulder. How could I feel so isolated and forsaken?

Still groggy from the bedtime medication they gave me, the nurses had to prod me awake at 6:00 a.m. "Sorry, but we need to prep you for surgery, Mrs. Bigliardi."

Kelly arrived just as two hefty orderlies lifted me onto a gurney. As they wheeled me down a maze of corridors, the

28

ceiling lights and the narrow hallways rushed past creating a surrealistic impression on my deadening senses. An elevator door opened, and Kelly followed a few steps behind.

One of the orderlies attempted to be lighthearted, joking about waking me up to put me to sleep again. Kelly tried to smile, but he looked uncomfortable, his hands jammed in his pant pockets, his shoulders slightly slumped forward.

Suddenly the elevator stopped and the door opened. A sign above double doors read: O.R. #1. Unable to enter this world with me, Kelly waved good-bye, and we smiled weakly at each other. "Catch you later," I called as the doors closed.

The orderlies pushed the gurney close to the wall and set the brake. My eyes had difficulty focusing, my speech was slurred and I was forced to trust the professionals around me. But inside I feared their human fallibility. What if something went wrong? Periodically someone lifted my wrist to check my identification band. When asked my name I mumbled, "Take your pick, my mother called me Patty, my friends call me Pat, but I like Patricia."

"We just wanted to know what you'd respond to in the recovery room," a masked nurse answered. I felt foolish. I didn't know why I'd given such a ridiculous answer.

I became aware that others lay on gurneys around me, all strangers. Our bodies draped with crisp white sheets, heads covered with green caps, our faces obscured from one another because we were flat on our backs, we shared a significant moment in time. Each of our lives would soon be altered in some permanent way.

I wondered why they were there. What was their secret?

Finally wheeled into the operating room, I immediately noticed the lowered temperature. The cold caused me to shiver uncontrollably. "May I have a blanket?" Masked faces loomed above me. Their voices were friendly, but

their covered heads and hidden faces accentuated my vulnerability. They lifted me from the gurney to a narrow, hard operating table. I saw a small tray on a stand with surgical instruments laid precisely side by side.

The large overhead theater lights, hooded in sparkling stainless steel, reflected cold reality. My thoughts drifted into neutral. I floated in and out of sleep.

"We're ready, doctor."

Dr. Poppy was moving toward me.

"Okay, let's begin. How are you doing, Pat?"

"Fine, I think." His familiar voice was the only thing that reassured me before the room went black.

"Patricia, Patricia, wake up." The nagging voice pushed against my consciousness. Only my eyelids were able to move. An older women stood next to my bed. "You're in the recovery room. How are you feeling?"

My tongue felt stuck to the roof of my mouth. "I'm so thirsty . . . I'd like some water."

My body felt heavy as if it were pressed against the mattress by a weight. Slowly the lights grew dim. I sank into the deep, dark hole of unconsciousness again.

"We're going to take you back to your room now, Pat. Ready?" My eyes glanced up toward the clock on the wall with the big black numbers. It said one o'clock. Two husky young orderlies lifted me off the bed onto a waiting gurney. Once again I felt myself rolling through double doors, into an elevator, down endless corridors, and finally into my room. The bed next to mine was empty. I was grateful to be alone.

Slowly as I opened my eyes, a small, red, heart-shaped box came into focus. "Happy Valentine's Day, Mom." My

eyes moved up from the box to the smiling face of my son. "Hi, Champ," I mumbled, trying to return his smile.

My husband's voice cut in, "Pat, the nurses want you to try to stay awake. You're not going to be able to come home tonight if you don't start rallying." As I turned my face toward him I noticed a small vase of flowers in his hand. "We brought the smallest box of candy," he said, "fewer calories." I ignored his allusion to my weight.

"How nice of you to bring me flowers." My voice was flat, expressionless. Poor Kelly, I thought, always wanting a pat on the back for the obligatory gesture.

I drifted off again. I didn't want to wake up.

"We'll keep her here overnight." I recognized Dr. Poppy's voice. She isn't recovering from the anesthesia as well as we hoped, so we want to observe her for another twelve hours or so." They were talking about me as if I couldn't hear them.

"We're going home, Pat." My husband leaned down to whisper in my ear. "Dr. Poppy wants you to stay overnight again. We'll see you in the morning, okay?"

I nodded yes and attempted a smile to reassure my son I was doing fine. Inside I was anything but fine. I wanted to tell someone what had happened to me. But who could I tell? None of my friends knew the real reason I was here. I could feel the anesthesia beginning to wear off but my mind was still groggy. I wanted to float back into the world of black billowy clouds, a world void of pain.

"Are you ready to leave?" The next morning Kelly popped his head around the corner of the doorway before walking in.

"All packed, ready to hit the trail." I tried to sound up beat. It was 10:30 a.m.

31

"Why don't we stop for lunch on the way home, then I've got to get back to the office," Kelly said. "I'm leaving on a trip next week, so I've lots of stuff to get done before I go." He picked up my suitcase.

"Ready to be discharged, Mrs. Bigliardi?" A young aide had entered my room. She motioned to a wheelchair. "You'll have to take one of our chariots downstairs, it's hospital policy."

I smiled cheerfully at all the nurses and thanked them for their kind care. My arms held the Valentine candy box and flowers, but the aching emptiness was in my heart. The last time I left this hospital I'd held my newborn son in my arms.

We didn't say much on the way to the restaurant. Normally, Kelly would have dropped me off at home and rushed back to the office. He paused outside the restaurant to buy a newspaper.

We ordered our meals, then buried our heads behind newsprint. During lunch we talked casually about his job and the sales trip he'd be taking the following week.

But we never mentioned the surgery or our baby.

Kelly carried my suitcase into the house, set it down in the entry hall, then turned to head back to the car. "I need to get going, have to get back to the office. I probably won't be home until 7:30 or 8:00 tonight. I'll need to make up for the time I lost these past few days." His comment made me feel guilty for imposing on him.

I lay down on the family room couch. Deep waves of melancholy washed over me as I drifted in and out of sleep. Before I realized it, the afternoon had ebbed away and my son was home from school.

"Hi, Mom!" Little Kelly shouted his greeting as he burst through the front door. He reached down to hug me, "Dad and I missed you. Are you feeling okay?" His face

reflected concern. I stroked his hair and held his soft warm cheeks between my hands.

"Yes, honey, I'll be okay in just a few days," I reassured him, as I kissed his cheek.

A few weeks later I visited Dr. Poppy for my post-op exam.

"You're healing well," he said with a smile. "There isn't any reason why you can't have another child, but I think you should wait a few months before getting pregnant again."

I nodded my head. I'd never told him that my husband hadn't wanted this baby.

The days passed into weeks and I didn't consciously think about my abortion again.

INSIGHT QUESTIONS FOR CHAPTER 2

1. Where did your abortion take place? Describe any details of the abortion procedure you remember and any feelings you recall before, during, and after your abortion.

2. Were you aware of any physical, emotional, or spiritual changes that occurred following your abortion? Be specific.

3. Can you remember a time when your conscience tried to tell you that abortion was a wrong decision? How did you respond?

3
...

When the Fury
Cannot Be Spent

"Dry Creek Village, contemporary townhome living for the discriminate Santa Clara Valley home buyer," advertised the brochure. "Tennis courts, swimming pool, and recreation center are all available for your enjoyment in prestigious Willow Glen."

Santa Clara Valley lies 70 miles south of San Francisco. Once called the "Valley of Hearts Delight," it offered breath-taking vistas that unfolded each spring. Row upon row of prune and cherry trees burst forth with dollops of delicate pink, mauve, white and purple blossoms, which would have inspired the likes of a Monet or Renoir.

But those pastoral scenes were fading, yielding to a suburban infestation of tract houses and shopping malls.

Beyond the Hidden Pain of Abortion

Except in Willow Glen.

On its quiet, tree-shaded streets, a mixture of Tudors, Victorians, thatched-roof cottages, and stucco bungalows reflected a variety of by-gone eras typical of an older, more established neighborhood.

Flowers bloomed in rich palettes of crimson, fuchsia, violet, and sunburst yellow. Small antique shops, ethnic delicatessens with their distinctive odors and quaint boutiques dotted the four-block-long downtown area.

It was a place where roots went deep, a community that prided itself on long-term relationships. Old money resided in Willow Glen, and I needed to belong, to be counted among its ranks of prominent residents. We moved there in November.

The sign outside the pool gate read: "For Dry Creek Village Residents Only," its ring of exclusivity alluring and seductive. I unlocked the large wrought iron gate with my key. I hoped it would also lead to acceptance and position and the elusive contentment I'd strived for, which had always seemed beyond my reach.

"Marco." Eyes closed, a young boy in the pool cocked his head as he listened intently for a response. "Polo," cried out his companions who floated just beyond his reach. "Marco . . . Polo . . . Marco . . . Polo." Back and forth the sounds ricocheted off the pool deck. It was a game of water tag with a twist: the hunter, whose eyes had to be shut tight, could hunt only with his ears. Over and over again the young boy called out as he thrashed at the water in search of his prey. His companions laughed and screeched as they darted past, avoiding his grasp by mere inches.

Desperate for the ordeal to end, the hunter's arms blindly flailed through the air hoping to touch someone—anyone—so he could be, once again, part of the group.

36

When the Fury Cannot Be Spent

As I walked through the gate, the repetitive refrain grated against my senses. It was too close to my own life where a gray pallor fogged my inner world and made it difficult to see. Whenever I called, "Marco" and reached out for Kelly, no one answered. I was playing the game alone.

Lounge chairs set in straight rows stood like silent sentries around the edge of the pool. Small clusters of women chatted around tables whose bright striped umbrellas waited to be unfurled.

The chlorine in the air accosted my nose like the first sharp notes of reveille on the ear. As I stepped to the pool's edge and sniffed the water, I was 10 years old again at camp, waiting for swimming class to begin.

"Pat, Pat, come over and join us." Paula, my neighbor beckoned, interrupting my daydreaming,

"I'll be right there." I straightened up and waved in her direction.

Paula had already convened the afternoon confab.

Although I'd only known her a few months she was obviously the Grand Dame of the complex. It was evident her daily jaunts to the pool were the highlight of her day. Older than the rest of us, she was articulate, well-read, and her quick wit was laced with sardonic asides. She loved sharing hot tidbits with anyone who would listen.

"Grab yourself a lounge chair and sit with us." She waved her hand in a sweeping half circle, much like reigning nobility.

Despite being slightly overweight, Paula was always well dressed. A multi-colored, silk swim jacket hung loosely over her matching swimsuit. Her wide, floppy brim straw hat, and sun glasses camouflaged her stabbing one-liners.

Humor was her weapon of choice, a sharp two-edged sword that would embrace or exclude you. I felt fortunate to be included in her select clique.

"And how are we today?" I greeted the group, placing a large pitcher of Sangria, now my constant companion, on the table. "Kelly called from Chicago last night. It looks like he'll be gone for another four days." I poured my first glass. "Sometimes I have to pinch myself to make sure I'm still married." The whine in my voice made me wince inside.

I pulled up a chair and sat in the shadows, away from the glaring sun. The sweet smell of coconut oil hung thickly in the air.

"I don't know how you stand it, Pat. If Jeff traveled as much as Kelly does I'd go stir crazy," said Sue. Her husband, an anesthesiologist at a local hospital, was rarely gone for more than a few hours.

"That's why she spends so much time with us," quipped Paula. "You didn't think it was our tantalizing conversation, did you?"

Already a deep tawny color, Sue pulled herself up just enough to lean on her elbows, the untied top to her two piece swimsuit threatening to slip off her thin, almost anorectic body. She deliberately dropped her chin so her designer sunglasses would slip down her nose. Peering over them she looked directly at me.

"And here I thought it was because we were such scintillating company."

"Ladies, ladies, ladies, what would I do without our little afternoon get-togethers? How much shopping, errands, and cooking can one person do? Unless. . . ." I gestured in Sue's direction, "I was like Sue here, our shopper's shopper!" I leaned forward, out of the shadows. "Where were you and Jeff this weekend, anyway?"

"We decided to take a quick jaunt down to Beverly Hills." Her throaty voice mimicked, "*Ve vonted* to be alone. . . ."

With one languid finger Sue slowly pushed her sunglasses back over her eyes and laughed. "The first day we were married I asked Jeff where he wanted me to develop my expertise, the kitchen or the bedroom? He said the bedroom, so I decided right then and there to always look good and to be good in bed." We all laughed. "But of course, we *did* do a little shopping!" she added coyly.

We laughed again.

Sue sat up excitedly, "Wait until you see the new outfit I bought at this cute little boutique on Rodeo Drive." Glasses off now, she continued, "Jeff insisted I get it, so who was I to resist?" She raised her eyebrows in innocence and shrugged her shoulders.

I envied Sue and her husband Jeff their well-defined marriage. Their expectations of each other were clear, and from all appearances, satisfying. The meter of their relationship was steady and dependable, a far cry from mine and Kelly's.

Piqued by my inability to boast of a spontaneous gift or weekend getaway, I felt resentment creep into my heart. Kelly's and my relationship resembled a movie set: we may have looked good on the outside, but turn the corner and it was empty behind the facade.

Still, we both were trying in our own way to salvage a marriage that was reeling from the aftereffects of adultery, separation, and a failed business.

I broke in on Sue's monologue.

"Kelly assured me the extensive traveling he's had to do will be over soon. We should know within 90 days if the venture capital money his company is looking for comes through."

I wanted to impress them, to have them believe Kelly's position was significant. In reality he hated his job. "I'm living a life of quiet desperation," he said in a moment of

truth. He longed to be the C.E.O. of his own company again. He hoped by doing double duty as both temporary regional sales manager and operations manager he would propel himself into a key position with this firm and make enough to start his own business.

Paula's voice interrupted my thoughts.

"What do you think about President Ford's having a female vice-presidential candidate?"

"I think it would be political suicide," Sue said quickly.

"What do you think, Pat?"

My hands were busy rubbing suntan lotion on my legs. "You know I went back to college in 1972 and planned to go to law school after getting my B.A., in political science. I wanted to be the first female senator from the state of California." I laughed self-consciously. "But I don't think the public is ready for a female vice-president." I screwed the cap back on the tube and tossed it on my towel. "Not yet anyway."

"I bet you would be good in politics."

"Why would she want to do that? This women's liberation thing is going to do more harm for women than good." Sue examined her new Juliette fingernails, holding one hand, then the other out in front of her. "I like my life. Jeff provides the money and I spend it." Laughter spun in the air once again.

In truth, my own beliefs had become ambivalent. On one hand, I'd touted the women's liberation message for years. Prompted by a need to feel valued and respected by my husband, I strived to have a career especially during our 15 months of separation.

On the other hand, I wanted to stay home to provide my son with the same secure feelings I had growing up. My skills as a wife and mother, however, were not valuable commodites to my husband.

Recently, television talk shows agreed with Kelly.

"By the way, I've been meaning to ask you how you were feeling. Any repercussions from your surgery a few months ago?" Paula curled back the brim of her sunhat to look at me.

"I didn't know you had surgery." Sue's voice showed concern.

"Oh, I'm fine now." I rose swiftly and walked to the Sangria pitcher, hoping my voice carried a tone of nonchalance. "I was having some minor gynecological problems, and my doctor thought a D & C might help."

Quickly, I turned the attention back in their direction. "Do either of you want some?" I poured myself a tall glass of the wine cooler, being sure to drop in some fresh orange slices and maraschino cherries.

"No Sangria for me. Too many calories, you know. Mustn't lose my appeal," Sue grinned, patting her concave stomach. "I'll stay with my dry white wine."

That evening the phone rang.

"How's everything at home?" Kelly's deep resonant voice reached through the phone and soothed my loneliness.

"I'm glad you called. We miss you." Lowering my voice I tried to evoke all the seductive warmth I could. I pictured his face, each fold, every plane and angle, the shadow of his brows, his olive complexion, the fullness of his lips. They had been objects of my close scrutiny and now I missed them all.

"How's Little Kelly? Has he gone to bed yet?"

"No, he's right here."

"Let me talk to him."

I handed the phone to our son, "It's Dad."

A few minutes later Little Kelly hung up.

"Dad said he had to go. He'll talk to you when he gets home next week."

41

It was then I realized Kelly had never intended to speak to me.

Only a few days before he left I found myself screaming at him. "How can we even begin to put this marriage back together if you're never here?" As I turned to face him, my reflection in the dressing room mirror caught me by surprise. My hair looked wild and unkempt, my eyes bulged with anger, my face was red and contorted from the spasm that constricted my throat.

Why, why am I so angry?

This inner rage which seethed just below the surface of my emotions would catch me off-guard, exploding without warning. I didn't know where it came from or why it happened or even when it would occur next. But like a rogue wave surging soundlessly toward the shoreline, it would smash against the jagged edges of my life without warning. Once spent, a heavy undertow of hopelessness dragged my shame back out to sea.

"We need you home, Kelly. Please try to slow down," I would plead.

"I can't, Pat, I just can't. There's too much for me to do." His customary silent withdrawal into his work-a-day world left me frustrated by my inability to convince him of *our* need for relationship.

A part of him thrived on the pressure of long hours at work. He seemed to excel when the tension increased. It was as if he needed the constant overload to keep the pace he'd set for himself. He floated in and out of my life, raising hopes of normalcy when he was home, but, like cotton candy, the sweetness dissolved the minute I tried to savor it.

What difference did it make to be married, I would ask myself. He's working such long hours that even when he

is home he's so tired we can hardly talk to one another. I can't remember the last time we were intimate.

We're drifting again like we did before he had his affair, I thought. Although I didn't tell anyone, I knew I was unable to control the inevitability of our future.

During this time, my mother became severely ill. One day she confessed that she was afraid of dying. I tried to comfort her, "Mom, come on, you've been a good person your whole life. If anyone's going to heaven, you are."

A few weeks later, I had a dream:

"Come on, Mom," I said, "come with me. I'll show you how great heaven is. You don't have to be afraid. Come up with me."

As we approached the tall iron fence surrounding heaven, we could see people were pressed together like at any cocktail party, holding wine glasses in their hands and chatting amiably. At the gate stood a short bespectacled black man dressed in a tan three piece suit. A thin gold chain dangled from the watch fob tucked in his vest pocket.

He nodded as if he recognized me.

Somehow I realized this man was waiting for us.

"We're not here to stay," I said as we got closer. "I'm just showing my mother how wonderful heaven is so she won't be afraid to die."

"Your mother is welcome here." His dark eyes held mine in a solemn gaze, "But you can't come in."

My smile vanished. "Why, why can't I come in?"

His eyes never shifted from my face, "Because you're a murderer."

Instantly I felt the certainty of the alternative. A death chill spiraled through me. *If I can't go to heaven, then I'm going to hell.*

Panic propelled me to claw toward consciousness. *My*

Beyond the Hidden Pain of Abortion

God, I'm going to hell! "It's just a dream," I kept repeating to myself. But locked in a small crevice of my mind, out of reach and beyond my ability to rationalize, the truth of my fear haunted me.

"Fires Plague Parched Santa Clara Valley" heralded the newspaper headline. The record breaking, 100-degree June heat wave continued to smother the city.

Kelly was trying to keep more regular hours even if his 60-hour work week left him too exhausted for much beyond the mundane routine of dinner, some conversation about the office, and an occasional evening of television.

Lately, he had complained about the tension that existed between Gary, a chemical engineer, and a young female biochemist, Naomi, who headed the research operations.

One evening, he walked in the door and announced, "I've invited Gary, you know, the guy who works in the research lab, to come to dinner next Thursday."

I was surprised. I didn't know why Kelly chose to invite Gary to dinner, but I was curious to see what would come of it. He hadn't invited anyone home since we'd moved there in November.

"Do you want me to cook anything special?"

"No, just a nice roast or something. You know, don't make a big deal over it." It was his not so subtle way of saying don't spend too much money.

But the prospect of having one of his colleagues to dinner excited me. I could pull out all my culinary skills and flaunt my intellectual prowess. This would be an elegant evening that would make my husband proud of me. Yes, that's what I would make it!

On Tuesday, I spent an hour rummaging through my closet to find just the right outfit, casual but elegant. Then I poured through my favorite cookbooks. Each recipe I

chose became a *tour de force* in my mind's eye.

The dinner menu would begin with hors d'oeuvres of stuffed mushrooms and baked brie cheese smothered in toasted almonds, served with white wine in the living room. After polite conversation we would move to the dining room. A mixed green salad served with herb bread would be followed by tiger prawns swimming in garlic wine sauce.

The main course, accompanied by a mellow cabernet, would be prime rib served with fresh asparagus and baked potatoes. Then the dessert *piece de resistance*, flaming cherries jubilee!

Thursday arrived and I was feverishly involved in preparing for my party. Bouquets of fresh cut flowers were placed discreetly around the living and dining room.

Promptly at 7:00 p.m. I greeted Gary at the door in my green silk shirt and slacks. His unkempt, bushy hair, wrinkled shirt and polyester bell-bottom pants made him look more like a '60s dropout than a chemical engineer. Only his plastic pocket protector hinted at his occupation.

After the three of us exchanged pleasantries during cocktails, Kelly's and Gary's conversation centered on business. They picked at my hors d'oeuvres. When we moved to the dining room, I sat in silence across the table and watched them eat. They could as well have been at MacDonalds.

"Gary, when do you think you'll have the phase one diagnostic chips ready?"

"Any day now. Although our schedule has slipped, with all the overtime we've been putting in, I think we'll make our deadlines."

Kelly kept prodding Gary. In charge of the sales effort, he'd been concerned that the conflict between Gary and Naomi caused delays in the already tight schedule. If the

product's debut was postponed it could mean disaster for the start-up company.

As the meal ended, Gary grew bored with Kelly's all business attitude and tried to include me in their discussion. It was obvious he had hoped Kelly's invitation meant an interest in friendship, but he concealed his disappointment.

"I guess you've gathered by our conversation, IDT is a pressure cooker, a hell-of-a place to work," he said to me. "But I don't suppose I'm telling you anything new, considering Kelly's 100-hour weeks."

Kelly's retort was quick and sharp. "Don't give her any more ammunition than she already has."

I attempted conciliation. "He's been making an effort to be home more lately, honest."

By now the wine had relaxed Gary. His inhibition had fled and he leaned back in his chair. "I'll tell you someone who's driven, it's that Naomi. I swear she has ice in her veins. Man, she has come close to putting me over the edge a number of times. She's one bitchy lady, excuse my French, Pat."

Kelly had mentioned Naomi several times during our conversations about the office staff. Although born and raised in Japan, she had been educated at the University of California, Berkeley. Her position as head of research was unique for a woman and she had a reputation for being a hard taskmaster. I envied the respect Kelly had for her.

At the company Christmas party in December, my encounter with Naomi left a distinct aftertaste. Watching her face as she extolled my husband's virtues, I suspected she wished he were single.

"I don't like you talking about her that way." Kelly's rebuff jolted me. "You have your problems with her, but I see her as a hard working, committed person."

"Come on, Kelly, you know as well as I do she can be

46

hell-on-wheels. Admit it," Gary pressed.

"I don't want you bad-mouthing her in front of me, is that clear?" The harshness of Kelly's reprimand made me feel embarrassed for Gary. He was obviously taken aback by the strength of Kelly's defense of Naomi. So was I.

Why is he so defensive? It hit an all too familiar chord, but I wasn't ready to acknowledge the surge of suspicion just yet.

By July, my days were running together. At mid-morning I left behind the unraveling threads of my life strewn carelessly about the house: piles of laundry, stacks of unfinished paperwork, and I headed down to the pool.

One morning, as I unlocked the pool gate, I noticed a young girl at the far edge of the water. The distance between us didn't dull the almost translucent glow that seemed to radiate from her. A quick, easy smile crossed her face frequently, and her laugh was full and infectious as she chatted with her friends. For several moments I watched her quietly. I felt myself yearning to experience her youthful vitality once again.

I used to look just like that when I was her age, I thought. Watching her, I realized how numb I'd become. My feelings were trapped beneath the gray cloud that hovered over me, dulling the colors of my life.

As I continued to watch her joy, the encounter made me aware of my growing cynicism. It oozed through thousands of tiny feeder veins tainting every aspect of my existence.

My eyes stayed riveted on her.

Somehow in an instant I knew. *Why, she's alive with life, that's it, isn't it?* I felt a growing anguish as I watched her. *I've lost hope, that's it. I'm no longer sure that things can get better.* Inside, deep inside, I was dying and I could smell the stench.

47

Kelly surprised me on our eleventh wedding anniversary. He took the July 31st weekend off and took me to Carmel. We stayed at the Highlands Inn, long a romantic hideaway on a Big Sur cliff overlooking the Pacific Ocean. For two days, my spirits revived.

Once we got back home, however, we slipped back into the same old cycle of anger and accusation. I searched for a way to draw his attention back to me, back to the love we once felt so passionately, but my language was now foul with a growing bitterness. That, and my drinking drove him further and further into his career.

One night in September, Kelly was already in bed when I began my lament as I undressed. He slapped his magazine down.

"If you'd find something constructive to do instead of playing the self-indulgent spoiled brat with your gossiping friends, you wouldn't need me so much." His eyes glared at me. "Do something with your life, Pat."

"You're just trying to avoid your responsibilities," I lashed back as I picked up my glass. "You love all the cheers for your self-imposed sacrifice, but you're just a damned workaholic. Admit it!" I felt my face flush, but my mouth wouldn't stop.

"I'm beginning to feel like I've joined a convent. I can't even remember when we made love last. When are we going to start enjoying the pleasure of being married?"

"Since when was marriage a pleasure?" he snapped.

I reeled around. "Maybe things would change if you were home more," I shouted. "Are you really working or have you started another affair?" My unleashed fury knew no bounds now. I wanted to tear at his heart just as he'd ripped mine. "At least consider our son. He needs two parents, not a single mother!"

The man in front of me turned into stone. His facial

48

features were set like hardened clay, his arms crossed tightly in front of him. The light left his dark brown eyes. Silence.

Without a word, he got out of bed, dressed, and walked downstairs. I heard the front door open, shut, and the dead bolt lock in place.

INSIGHT QUESTIONS FOR CHAPTER 3

1. Do you find yourself over-reacting to everyday problems? Do you feel a constant sense of sorrow just below the surface of your emotions?

2. Do you experience bursts of rage out of proportion to what the situations warrant? Describe a particular incident.

3. What have been some of the results of your expression of anger?

4. Describe the way your father dealt with anger. Describe how your mother dealt with it. How did you feel when they expressed their anger toward you?

5. How would you like to express your anger differently?

6. Is there anything about your abortion that you are angry about?

4
...
Beckoned
from Silence

The gray January sky outside my bedroom window mirrored my mood. My son left for school and I struggled to face another day. *Has it been three months since Kelly walked out on our marriage?* I felt as if a large clawed hand had reached in and ripped my heart out.

Over and over the final scene played out in my mind. One evening in October after another blowout, it happened. "This is it, we can't continue to live like this," Kelly was adamant. "We're hurting our son and one another. Either you leave or I will."

"I'm not going anywhere," I answered defiantly. "If you want to leave, do it." As I spoke, a sick, panicky feeling crawled over me.

Kelly continued, "We've been trying to work on this for

months, maybe some time away from each other will help." I sensed a hint of hope in his voice. "But I don't see why I always have to be the one to leave. Why don't you move out this time?"

"I don't think separation is the answer, so why should I leave?" I demanded insolently. I had a sinking feeling that if I were to go, he'd never allow me to return.

"Face it, Pat, our constant fighting isn't accomplishing anything." The eyes I loved were shutting me out. He sighed, his voice devoid of the hope I heard moments before. "I'm not even sure I want to work it out, not now anyway." He turned on his heel and went up the stairs. A few minutes later he was back, suitcases in hand. He kissed Little Kelly, said goodbye, and left.

In November, my parents and two sisters had flown to California from Michigan, hoping to help Kelly and me reconcile our marriage. But after talking to my husband for eight solid hours one day, Dad's advice startled me.

"Forget him, Pat. You need to file for divorce and start again." My father's penetrating *Calabreze* Italian eyes belied his tender spirit.

My parents' relationship, often volatile, had teetered more than once on the brink of disaster. But no matter how difficult it got, their determination to stay together enabled them to grow past their wounds. Dad didn't believe in divorce. It wasn't easy for him to say advise me this way.

"Life is tough," Mom would say. "Sometimes it seems some problems are more than you can handle, but the only way to solve them is to work through them together."

Now, on this gray morning at the beginning of 1977—a new year, I rolled over and bunched up my pillow. I could hear Dad's voice ringing in my ears.

"The problem, as I see it, is neither you nor Kelly have

humbled yourselves before God," he said, shaking his head in sorrow. He paced slowly around the family room, "You don't attend church, and you've made no attempt to include spiritual values in your lives. The only topics of conversation I ever hear around here are how much money you're going to have and how successful Kelly's business is going to be." His voice reflected disappointment at our priorities. "You're too busy trying to impress your so-called friends.

"Well, daughter, there is a whole lot more to life than having money and possessions." Whenever he used the term *daughter* I knew he was about to reprimand me. "You're both too spoiled—determined to have your own way at any cost." Again he slowly shook his head, his full head of coal black hair still glistening. "You've almost destroyed each other and your son."

He looked around at the lavishly appointed family room then looked directly at me, lowering his voice to emphasize his point. "The price you've paid in pain and suffering for that obstinacy has been much too high."

My father's words hung in the air like a sword of truth. But I wasn't ready to receive another wound to my pride. "I know you're right, but I do love Kelly," I insisted. "I want our marriage to work."

"It may be too late for that." He spoke deliberately. "But you do have a son to think about." His black eyes bored into me, "You need God in your life, Pat. He's your only hope."

His words were painful to hear, yet they penetrated my headstrong resistance. Dad was right, I had to stop running and get my own life in order. I had a son who needed me now more than ever.

I gave my pillow another punch as my memories drifted back to my freshman year at Central Michigan University. That was when I started to play hooky from Sunday morning services.

Beyond the Hidden Pain of Abortion

Away from my parents' watchful eye for the first time, I did what many young people do, slipped into self-indulgence and called it religious freedom. Proud of my intellect I decided religion was fine for others who needed an emotional crutch, but it wasn't a necessary part of my life.

Months passed before remorse set in. Then one Friday evening just before spring break, I decided to go to confession—to start afresh.

My resolve to seek God grew deeper as I walked the few blocks from campus to old St. Mary's near town. Ascending the wide cement steps, I paused a moment before opening one of the massive twelve foot high doors which led to the narthex of the church. Why did I always feel a little frightened before I went in? Although I had attended church all my life, I still felt like a stranger once inside.

Taking a square lace mantilla out of my pocket I draped it over my head, dipped my fingers in the holy water, crossed myself, and genuflected just as I had done since childhood. A hint of incense mixed with the smell of burning wax lingered in the air.

Except for subdued lighting above the confessionals near the entrance and a few votive candles flickering in red glass holders at a side altar, the sanctuary was dark. Mahogany pews, polished to a rich luster, reflected the warm glow of the candle light. The hollow sound of a coin dropping into a tin box echoed off the tiled floor.

A high pitched Gothic ceiling with its exposed hand carved wooden beams and vibrant stained glass windows set at the front of the nave drew my eyes up, skyward. I found my thoughts move from my own awkwardness to the awesome awareness of the infinite.

As I knelt down to wait my turn in the confessional, I could feel a lump begin to form in my throat. An unexpected sense of sadness enveloped me. At first a few tears

54

welled up in my eyes, then began to spill down my cheeks.

My reaction surprised me. I rarely cried. But in the solitude of the expansive sanctuary, I realized how much I missed being there. In those brief moments another unexpected feeling brushed against my consciousness; I was aware of God's sorrow at my absence.

By the time I entered the small, dark cubicle, with its privacy screen, my heart was broken by the sorrow I felt about my apathy. When the priest pulled back the small wooden partition to hear my confession, I couldn't speak. Rather, I cried deep sobs of regret.

"What's the matter?" There was concern in his voice.

"Oh, Father, I've sinned." Unable to stop the sobs that rose from the depth of my being, I startled the old parish priest.

"Are you pregnant?" His question held a reproving tone.

"No!" I was stunned. I didn't have a boyfriend, for that matter. I grew more embarrassed at my inability to stop crying.

"Well, have you slept with a boy, then?"

"No," I moaned. The priest was silent.

"Well then, what have you done?" His voice bounced around in the small cubicle.

I gulped down a sob, "I haven't been to church in months, and I know I've disappointed God."

"You haven't been going to church? That's it?" It was evident the priest was confounded. I could hear his body shifting in his seat. "My young woman, get hold of yourself," he began. "Of course, you should be attending Mass, but that's no reason to get hysterical." He cleared his throat and leaned closer. "Are you sure there isn't anything else you want to confess?"

"No." I answered meekly, too ashamed to say anything else.

55

"All right then, as your penance say five 'Our Father's' and five 'Hail Mary's' and start going to Mass every week. I absolve you of your sins."

I left the confessional emotionally spent. Just a few minutes before I had dramatically felt God's presence, now I simply felt alone. Dejected, I knelt down to do my penance. The vast emptiness of the sanctuary echoed around me.

Dutifully I began to recite the words I learned as a child, "Our Father which art in heaven, . . ." I couldn't bring myself to finish the rote prayers I was asked to repeat. I wanted to believe in God, but if He was real He seemed too far away to reach.

It was then I felt the prick, the first injection of cynicism enter my heart. I simply rose and left the church. And I never attended Mass on a regular basis again.

The ticking of the clock next to my bed brought me back to the present. The dial said 11:30 a.m. and the gray of morning was lifting. I pulled my stiff body out of bed.

Reaching in to turn on the shower, I glanced in the mirror. My face was puffy and the dark patches under my eyes shouted fatigue.

Fear and anxiety were my constant companions now. How could we have started with so much hope, so much love only to end up just another divorce statistic? When we reconciled more than two years ago, Kelly asked me to put my trust in him again. He said he'd never leave us like he had before. Now I felt betrayed once again.

Stepping into the shower I replayed my father's warning. "Pat, you need God in your life, you'll never succeed in marriage, or life for that matter, without Him." Standing under the hot water did little to remove the cold chill of being divorced. Dare I reach out again to search for a God

whose distance seemed so insurmountable?

Still, trying to run life my way wasn't working. My pride, willfulness and cynicism brought nothing but pain and irreparable harm to everyone I loved. I had to admit I'd reached the end of my rope and still didn't have any answers.

As the hot water pulsated against my body, unabated tears began to course down my face. I heard my voice cry out, "God, if You're real, please, please reveal Yourself to me." Then, as a gesture of surrender, I did the only thing I could think of to do.

"I baptize myself in the name of the Father, and of the Son, and of the Holy Ghost," I said with determination in my voice.

The water continued to flow in the same rhythmic cadence, against the glass shower door. There wasn't a flash of light or a booming voice that spoke to me; outwardly nothing changed. But I could feel my muscles begin to relax. The inner tension I held rigidly in place for years poured down the drain with the water that swirled beneath my feet. In its place, I felt the strange, almost alien, sensation of peace embrace me.

I stood motionless, letting the water wash over me until it ran cold. Stepping out of the shower, I dried myself off, and slipped back into bed. Exausted, totally spent, finally I was able to rest. As I drifted off, I resolved to attend Mass the next week. This time I was determined to learn more about God.

"It's time to get ready, we'll have to leave for Mass in about 45 minutes."

Kelly groaned. "Do we have to go, Mom? We never went to church when Dad lived with us."

"I know honey, but I think it will be good for us."

Beyond the Hidden Pain of Abortion

Awkward and shy, once the service was over, I headed purposefully toward my car. Regulars stood in the parking lot, chattering about the past week with each other as children ducked and dodged through the crowd.

I realized how uninformed I was about spiritual matters, but I felt good about my new resolve. I didn't know how to incorporate God into our lives, but I knew this time I'd keep searching. For the first time in years I felt a few strands of hope begin to weave back into my life.

Three weeks later, the first light of dawn broke across my window. "Dear God," I prayed, "I need to know more about You. Please guide me, show me what I'm supposed to do."

After dropping Little Kelly off at school, I headed for a bookstore. Books had always been my solace in times of despair. Within their pages I found answers to questions without fear of being labeled ignorant or silly. Was there a guidebook to the truths I so desperately sought? Perhaps there was an author who could point me in the direction I needed to go.

I peered inside *Books, Inc.*, a familiar haunt of mine. Aisle upon aisle of books touted every subject imaginable. Opening the door I looked for a section I hadn't explored in years, Religion and Philosophy.

My eyes meandered across the rows of book jackets. *A Man Called Peter* by Catherine Marshall caught my eye. I recognized that title, but why? Pulling it from the shelf I realized I'd seen the movie. I remembered how I'd been drawn to watch it every time it was on TV. It had an almost magnetic power about it. How strange to find this book today, I thought. Quickly I purchased it and headed home. I couldn't wait to read it.

With Kelly in school, I was free to crawl back into bed

and snuggle up with my new found treasure. Marshall's writing captured my attention immediately.

People today wonder about this matter of God having a detailed plan, a blueprint, for each individual in the universe. "If there is really a God," they ask, "and if He is interested in me, how do I go about getting in touch with Him? How does He talk to people today?"[1]

There it was, the very question for which I sought an answer! I read on with the rush of passion. The morning hours passed quickly. Startled by the phone, I was surprised to hear my husband's voice at the other end.

"How are you doing?" he asked casually.

"I'm okay. How are you?" I replied.

"Do you have anything planned for tonight?"

"No," I answered, a ray of hope lifting my spirits. "What's up?"

"I wanted to know if I could come by," he hesitated, "I need to serve you with the divorce papers."

A sick feeling gripped the pit of my stomach.

"Rolf will be with me. I didn't want you to receive them from an impersonal process server, so we'll both be there around eight o'clock. How does that sound?"

Stunned by the prospect of seeing one of our friends in such painful circumstances was overwhelming. How could he ask me to do this? I could hardly bring myself to answer. I couldn't breathe.

"Is this necessary?" I finally asked.

"If tonight isn't a good night, then when would it be convenient?" he asked, ignoring my real question.

His businesslike manner pressed me to maintain my own composure. But I wanted to scream, "Don't do this,

please don't destroy everything. Please say you love me, please don't leave us. We love you, Kelly. Your son and I are lost without you."

Instead, I answered, "Tonight is as good a night as any, I suppose."

His relief was palpable. "We'll see you then, I've got to get back to work."

Hanging up the phone, anger swept over me. *How can he do this?* He sounded so aloof, almost happy. If he could only see my heart, or Little Kelly's face when he asked if his daddy would be coming back someday, maybe then he'd rethink his decision. But I sensed that nothing would deter him this time.

At precisely eight-thirty the doorbell rang. I headed downstairs. I'd painstakingly dressed, then stood behind my make-up and a false demeanor of composure for the occasion.

As I descended the stairs I was surprised that Kelly had already unlocked the door *of my home* to let Rolf and himself inside. They stood together looking up at me smiling as if we were all headed out for the evening.

"Hi, Rolf, long time no see," I said trying to be cordial. I walked over to hug him as I had so many times in the past. Over six-feet-two inches, with blond hair and vibrant blue eyes, he reached down and placed his arm around me.

"How are Linda and the kids?"

"Pretty good, getting bigger everyday." His Norwegian accent wrapped me in a blanket of familiarity.

Rolf looked me in the eyes before he lowered them sheepishly, "I'm sorry I'm here under these circumstances."

I smiled in appreciation for his sensitivity. "Well, I guess I'm glad it's someone I know."

Kelly smiled self-consciously. He handed me a stack of papers, then jammed his hands into his pockets.

Rolf said something to me. I suspected it was part of California's legal procedure of having two people serve divorce papers, but my mind didn't allow me to hear the words.

I could see both men's mouths moving, their lips forming words, but it was as if an invisible shield had been lowered between us.

Their facial expressions and body movements seemed to be in slow motion. I heard faint, skittish laughter, the sound muffled and elongated as if it were funnelling up from a deep tunnel.

Then Kelly's voice broke through. "We need to get going."

"Dad, you just got here, don't leave," Little Kelly cried.

I'd forgotten my son was in the room watching.

"I'll be by tomorrow to pick you up for dinner, like we planned, Sport. Right now I've got to take Rolf home."

"But, Dad, I miss you." His big, sad brown eyes said more than words.

"I miss you too, Sport. But I'll see you tomorrow, okay?"

"Bye, Dad, I love you." His voice sought reassurance.

"I love you too, Son."

"Bye, Rolf, I guess I should say thanks," I said as I walked him to the door.

Rolf bent down to give me a hug. "Take it easy, Pat."

"I'll try." My lips pressed against my teeth in an awkward attempt to smile. I refused to allow myself to cry.

Kelly walked out the door, then turned back. "See ya."

I shut the door behind him.

I tucked Little Kelly into bed then sat down beside him.

"Mom and Dad love you, Kel." I stroked his head, smoothing out his rumpled hair.

Instantly tears filled his eyes. "Why does he have to leave, Mom?"

I leaned down to kiss his cheek. "I know it hurts, doesn't it?"

He sat up and wrapped his small arms around me, pressing his head against my chest.

"I miss him, Mom, I love Dad. I don't know why he has to live some place else."

"I know, Kel, I feel the same way, I miss him too."

I held him against me, wishing my body could draw his pain into me. How do you explain to an eight-year-old child, "Daddy doesn't love Mommy any more, but he'll always love you"? It didn't make sense to me, why did I expect it would to him?

Slowly I began to rock him back and forth. Finally his arms slipped down and his eyes closed as he rested in my arms. I waited until I knew he was asleep, then I gently laid him back down, resting his head on the pillow. I tucked the covers under his chin.

I stared at my little boy, so young and vulnerable. *Dear God, help me, give me the strength to raise him alone.* I felt so frightened by the responsiblity that lay before me. I leaned down and kissed him once again, I couldn't help but wonder what the failure of our marriage would breed in him. I turned to leave but glanced back to take one more look at his smallness before turning off the light.

My own body was heavy from exhaustion. Mechanically I prepared for bed. Slipping between the covers, I noticed Catherine Marshall's book on my night stand. Automatically I picked it up and began to read.

The practical ramifications of the fact that "God is Love" began to dawn on me. I knew that anything unloving in me, any resentment, unforgiveness, or

impurity shut out God, just as a muddy windowpane obscures the sunlight. Painfully, in an agony of mind and spirit, I began thinking back over my life recalling all too vividly all my transgressions and omissions.[2]

Marshall's words could have been my own. My mind began to scan the years of our marriage. Many times resentment and unforgiveness blocked the love Kelly and I once had for each other.

With tears manifesting the reality of what I was doing, I lay in bed and prayed, "Lord, I've done everything I've known how to do, and it hasn't been good enough. I'm desperately weary of the struggle of trying to persuade You to give me what I want. I'm beaten, whipped, through."[3]

I, too, felt completely beaten, defeated. It seemed no matter how hard I tried, I kept failing at the one thing I wanted most in my life.

It was well past midnight before I set the book down again.

Sleepily, I reached over to turn out the light. Although the event of the evening was more than I could fathom at the moment, Marshall's book had brought a sense of tranquility.

"Dear God," I began, "I forgive Kelly. I know he doesn't realize what he's doing. And, God, I'm beaten, and weary too. I give my life, however meaningless it may have been, to You." I closed my eyes and drifted off to sleep.

Sometime in the middle of the night a loud clap awakened me. Opening my eyes, I saw a white, glowing figure standing next to my bed, illuminating one side of the room. I raised myself up to a sitting position. Was I

dreaming? I blinked. But every time I opened my eyes, the light moved closer. It completely engulfed me.

A warmth poured over me like thick oil, soothing and satisfying. It was love—that's what I was feeling. It penetrated every fiber of my being. Somewhere in my consciousness I knew this was God. He was standing there, pouring His love through me without restraint. Complete. Boundless. Lavishly, it embraced me.

Then, soundlessly, peace wrapped its arms around me and slowly lowered me back onto the bed. As gently as it had come, the light receded. The glow of its presence lingered like the warmth of a father's arms.

I slipped into a deep, serene sleep.

After Little Kelly left for school, I stood at the kitchen sink pondering the events of the night before.

The afterglow of God's presence was still with me. I had never believed in mysticism, and I knew many of my friends would dismiss my "mystical" experience as a result of the stress I was under.

I understood that what had taken place was an encounter with the one true God, the God of my father, the God of my youth. Still powerless to find adequate words, I tucked my secret into my heart.

A short while later, a persistent impression kept bumping around in my brain, "Get a Bible."

Although I often debated the claims of the Bible I'd never read it. After church on Sunday, it was my family's tradition to sit around my parents' large kitchen table while Dad challenged us with thought-provoking questions. Inevitably the discussion would twist and turn toward God and the life style He required of us. Often Dad would get us to bring out the Bible to settle a dispute, but I had never read it on a consistent basis.

Suddenly I had an earnest desire to read its concepts and hear its words.

I decided to drive to a nearby Christian bookstore. Fearful my ignorance would shout accusingly before me, I approached the door timidly, like a stranger in alien territory.

Placing a mask of assurance on my face I swung the door wide with bogus confidence. I headed directly to the bookshelves as if I knew exactly where to find what I was looking for.

Half an hour passed while I roamed through the aisles in search of the section containing Bibles. Finally, horrified, I discovered they were behind a long counter only accessible to the sales staff. I would be forced to ask for help.

I approached the counter. An older woman with graying hair, her blouse neatly buttoned at the collar, came to my assistance.

"May I help you?" she asked politely.

"Yes, I'd like to buy a Bible."

"What kind of a Bible are you looking for?"

There are different kinds of Bibles? My unease was edging into panic.

"I'm looking for a Catholic Bible." I forced myself to sound assured.

"Oh?" She responded, with a slight tone of surprise in her voice.

"Would you prefer the *St. Joseph's Bible* or *The New American Bible*?"

Silence stood between us. She looked at me closely.

"*The New American Bible* has just been released. The language is easier to understand," she explained.

"Yes, that's the one I want." I answered in what I hoped was a confident manner.

"Do you want the complete Bible or the New Testament?"

65

I thought fast. I definitely wanted the latest edition, so I should probably take the newest testament.

"The new one, I'll take the newest one."

She looked a little puzzled but asked, "Would you prefer hardbound or paperback?"

I just want to buy a Bible! Short on funds I decided on the paperback version.

She rang up my purchase and I hastily retreated to my car.

Who would have guessed there would be so many questions to answer? My excitement overshadowed my chasm of ignorance, however. I could hardly wait to get home to begin my new journey of discovery.

The New American Bible, New Testament, read the cover. I approached it like any other book, opening it to chapter one, the "Book of Matthew." In the weeks that followed I read straight through to the end, "Revelation."

Many times during those weeks I found myself cynically questioning its passages. Yet, when I tried to put it down, sure that its claims were too far fetched to believe, a small voice reminded me of the night the light visited me. I could not explain or deny what had happened, so I moved past my doubts and accepted as truth what I was reading.

Parables I heard as a child were there as friends I hadn't visited in a long while.

> "What man of you, having a hundred sheep, if he loses one of them, does not leave the ninety-nine in the wilderness and go after the one which is lost until he finds it? And when he has found it, he lays it on his shoulder, rejoicing. And when he comes home, he calls together his friends and neighbors, saying to them, 'Rejoice with me for I have found my sheep which was lost!'" (Luke 15:4-6).

The familiarity of these parables brought a sense of stability I hadn't known in years. Not since I resided in my father's house had I felt the security that now surrounded me.

> "'You shall love the Lord your God with all your heart, with all your soul and with all your mind.' This is the first and great commandment. And the second is like it: 'You shall love your neighbor as yourself'" (Matt. 22:37-39).

When I didn't understand the concepts and principles, I used Peter Marshall's sermons as doors to understanding the heart of God:

> When faced with problems that worry us, we should, by all means, talk them over with the Lord.
> We should, because He wants us to turn the matter over to Him.
> But God may insist on bringing up other matters as a prerequisite of His answering our prayers.[4]

God was no longer a distant and disinterested deity. My personal encounter with the living God, the words of the Bible, the teachings of Jesus, the sermons of Peter Marshall, and the writings of Catherine Marshall brought God close.

> God is a God of laughter, as well as of prayer . . . a God of singing, as well as of tears.
> God is at home in the play of His children. He loves to hear us laugh.[5]

Soon I was reading more of Catherine Marshall's books. Then I began to read the books listed in her bibliographies,

authors such as Hannah Whitall Smith, Elisabeth Elliot, C. S. Lewis, George Müller, and Brother Lawrence. I was aware of a vast cavern that existed within my mind. I couldn't seem to fill it fast enough. "As I pondered these things and read my Bible, I found that Jesus never refused anyone who came to Him asking help,"[6] wrote Catherine Marshall.

Was that true? Had Jesus helped everyone who asked? I went on a hunt to determine if what Marshall had written was accurate. It was!

As my hunger for the understanding I sought so many years before was finally being satiated, something else began to happen.

Each day, remorse for things I had done was also piqued. One morning, as my mind searched my past, my abortion came to my awareness.

Tears, then sobs broke forth like a bursting dam. "Oh my God, please forgive me," I cried silently. I was now so aware of the sadness I had caused Him by my selfishness and rebellion. Yet His compassion surrounded me. Where once there was guilt, now I felt forgiveness. How could He be so loving, so merciful as to forgive me of this?

Yet deep within the well of my being I knew I was forgiven. No longer soiled by the soot of sin my tears of bitterness became tears of cleansing. Cleansed, by God's love, how could I not love Him in return?

"Oh God," I cried, my arms stretched upward. "Your love knows no bounds. Will I ever fully comprehend your magnificence?"

INSIGHT QUESTIONS FOR CHAPTER 4

Is God real to you? If so, how do you perceive Him? Is He someone you can approach? Can you trust Him with your hurts?

1. Describe your spiritual background in a few words. Begin with, "When I was a child. . . ."

2. Did you believe in God when you had your abortion? Do you believe in God now?

3. Do you believe God loved you before your abortion? Do you believe He loves you now?

4. What was your relationship with God when you faced your crisis pregnancy? At the time of your abortion did you think God could "see" or "hear" you? Were you afraid to talk to God before your abortion? Do you feel free to talk to Him today?

5. Do you believe God can forgive you for having had an abortion? Do you believe God can still forgive you if you have had more than one abortion?

6. Describe the relationship you have with God today.

Beyond the Hidden Pain of Abortion

5
...

A Cracked Cistern Holds No Water

I have uncovered his secret places, and he shall not be able to hide himself (Jer 49:10).

The air was filled with excitement as the audience anticipated another fun-filled evening with the dynamic youth evangelist visiting our congregation.

I leaned back in my seat, relaxed and grateful for the opportunity to escape the demanding media deadlines I faced the following week. Over 11 years had passed since my life-changing encounter with God on that night in February.

My divorce had become final in August of 1977. I was able to reestablish my advertising and public relations career and sustain my son and myself in our townhome in Willow Glen.

Beyond the Hidden Pain of Abortion

We joined Christian Community Church, which became the hub of our lives. Excellent Bible teaching and supportive friendships helped us regain our emotional equilibrium.

But then a series of events forced a number of life style changes to take place.

In 1980 my once strong and stalwart father was diagnosed with terminal cancer. His care, too difficult for my mother in advanced stages of diabetes, forced them to move in with us.

Three months after his initial diagnosis, Dad died.

After my divorce, I had relied heavily on my father to guide me through the uncharted waters of business. His keen advice and rock-solid values were instrumental in helping me gain a sense of stability and security for my son and me.

We felt his loss deeply.

Six months later, Mom's failing health required open heart surgery. Complications due to her diabetes necessitated that she receive round-the-clock care for almost a year.

The demands of raising my teenage son and overseeing Mother's health needs forced me to make a career change. The high pressure demands and deadlines of my advertising career were more than I could handle.

Teaching at our local Christian high school allowed me more time for my family, I reasoned. However, it also brought a lower level of income. It became necessary to sell our townhome.

By 1985, the stress overwhelmed me. I had a heart attack, quite unusual for a young woman of 41. The year of recovery was difficult and challenging; I was again rebuilding my life.

Then, in 1986 my mother passed away. By that time, I

had started a small advertising business and Kelly and I were experiencing renewed financial stability. God's mercy and provision sustained us and helped me gain a new perspective on life. Slowly, all the props that once had been so important to me were removed. My priorities had changed drastically, but there were still old wounds that needed healing.

"Tonight, I want to begin this performance a little differently than I usually do," announced the stocky, young man with a shock of coarse reddish brown hair and a full red beard. John Muncie, the energetic young speaker with a fast-paced, multi-media presentation, had a dynamic way of arresting your attention from the moment he walked onto the stage. "I know you're here for a seminar on music, but I'd like to start with a short film first.

"My good friend, Melody Green, from Last Days Ministries has produced a unique film I believe I'm supposed to share with you." A low hum rippled across the room as the audience shifted in their seats.

The house lights lowered, the title came on, and the camera lens focused on a slender, dark haired woman who appeared on the screen. Melody Green, widow of popular recording star Keith Green, was well-known as an effective speaker and supporter of the pro-life movement. I had seen a number of pro-life films in the 11 years since my abortion. I sat forward so that I could focus my attention more thoroughly.

Her voice had a firm resolve as she began to speak. "The sights you are about to see may disturb you, but it's important for you to know what these babies actually looked like when their lives were taken from them." She then held up a still, delicate infant. "This fetus was less than five months when it was aborted."

My eyes beheld a perfectly formed human being. Tiny, only as big as the palm of her hand, yet complete.

I was moved by her tender manner as she held each infant with a reverence for the life it represented. Her voice faded away and my eyes enfolded each baby, a life cut short without provocation. Slowly the realization of what I was witnessing reached down inside of me and touched a pain I didn't know existed.

Behind me, a man, his voice barely audible, began to weep. As his sobs broke through my consciousness, I felt the muscles of my chest constrict. A sound began to rise from the core of my being. I knew if I opened my mouth, a piercing, prevailing, wail would reverberate throughout the room. Panic gripped me. If the sound escaped, it would forever expose my shame.

I cupped my hand over my mouth and pressed my fingers tightly to my lips as if to push the scream back down my throat.

I wanted to get out of there! I wanted to run as fast as I could, to escape before I lost control.

Finally the house lights came up. Why, why was I in so much pain? For the rest of the evening I was able to push my questions to the back of my mind, but a pallor hung over me. I knew a significant event had occurred, and there were questions that needed answers, questions I didn't want to ask.

Just then, my strapping six-foot-tall son approached me. "What did you think of the film John showed, Mom? Those were incredible shots, awesome don't you think?"

"Yes they were pretty powerful. I don't think I've ever seen anything quite like them before." I distanced myself from what really had happened to me earlier in the evening. How could I ever tell my 19-year-old son what I had done so long ago?

The bright headlights cut across the early morning darkness. My wipers slowly swept across the windshield, pushing away the intermittent mist from the coastal fog which rolled in during the night. Shivering from the dankness, I pondered the events of the evening before.

What happened last night? I know I'm forgiven. God forgave my abortion 11 years ago. Why did I have such an adverse reaction to that film? My car rolled through the glistening black streets toward the office.

Finally I gathered up the courage to ask the nagging question: I am forgiven, aren't I, Lord? A small quiet voice answered, "You're forgiven, Pat." And then came the answer to my nagging questions, "You've grieved your sin. but now it's time to grieve the loss of your baby."

My baby! The words penetrated the wall I had placed around my perception of my abortion. I never allowed myself to acknowledge the death of my baby until now. *Oh God, it was a baby, wasn't it? It was my baby.* I couldn't hold back my tears.

The truth was too much for my mind to comprehend. I could barely see the white lines along the street as tears spilled down over my cheeks. *My daughter.* The words had come so easily.

Sitting in my car, I tried to regain some composure before walking into the office. The Lord had stood beside me through other times of grief; I knew he wouldn't leave me now. The path would be strewn with debris from the past. The question foremost in my mind: would I have the courage to face my worst nemesis, myself?

The meeting had already begun in the brightly lit room of the small library. I saw the familiar faces of my support group gathered around a long table. Fledging writers, we gathered once a month to share our lives and to encourage

one another. Diane, our mentor, nurtured our attempts to communicate, soothing our own self-depreciating criticisms with words of inspiration. She believed in us. And we reveled in her advocacy.

Ruth, whose twinkling eyes and whimsical disposition belied her 60-plus years, sat to the left. Tamara and Sara, her teenage daughter, sat across the table. Paula, a young mother with five rambunctious children at home, readily admitted she attended the meetings more for the adult conversation than the teaching.

I slid into a seat at the far end of the table. "Pat, we're so glad you were able to join us tonight." Diane paused mid-sentence to greet me.

"Sorry I'm late."

Their beaming smiles wrapped me in a warm blanket of welcome. These were my friends. I felt accepted and loved by them. I trusted their compassionate understanding.

Diane was the first to recognize my writer's soul. More importantly, I had grown to value her spiritual wisdom and insight. She listened to my laments for two years and guided me with soft invitations to seek the truths of life by studying Scripture. Her faith in me and our friendship had brought a refreshing input into my life.

The evening usually began with a short teaching by Diane, followed by an open discussion with everyone participating, usually all at the same time.

When Diane finished that evening, I hesitated before I spoke up.

"Diane, something happened to me last night. And I wondered if it would be okay for me to ask for advice from the group?"

Although I knew these were my friends, I wasn't sure how they would respond to my confession. I gathered my courage and began.

"Eleven years ago, prior to my divorce, I had an abortion." My eyes lowered, I was too ashamed to look anyone in the face.

"Oh, Pat, I'm so sorry," murmured Diane softly. Her compassionate voice encouraged me to continue.

"Then, last night I had a reaction to a film that was shown at church. It was the closest experience I've ever had to hysteria. It took everything I had not to scream and wail as I watched a woman hold those tiny aborted babies."

My eyes filled with tears. Tamara reached over and placed her hand on mine.

"Those pictures were very graphic, Pat. Are you sure you're ready to talk about it?"

"Yes, if you don't mind. I really need to tell someone. Only a few people know about my abortion."

"We're here for you, honey. We can listen as long as you need us to," Ruth said affectionately.

Words of comfort and understanding drifted above the table and settled around me like pillows stuffed with soft downy feathers. When I was finished, Ruth, a teacher for over 20 years, began to speak cautiously.

"Pat, perhaps you should begin to journalize your experience. Write down all the memories that come to mind, and be sure to include any feelings you had then and how you feel about it now. It may help you sort out your thoughts and give you a means of expressing your pain."

I felt positive for the first time that day. Her suggestion provided direction and purpose.

"Journalize my experiences, that's a good idea. I hadn't thought of that."

Diane added, "Why don't you write down everything you can remember and bring it with you next month? We should all be praying for Pat this month. This will be a

difficult assignment for her. When we get together for our next meeting, Pat, you might want to share some of your journal entries with us."

Over the next few days I sat down each night with my journal in hand. Bit by bit I pieced my memories together. But finally I couldn't get past my written words, "So much anger, so much pain is inside of me." It would take me weeks before I finished that paragraph.

Each time I tried to remember what had occurred, my hand would shake. Fearful of releasing the rage, and uncertain as to what would happen if I allowed the pain to surface, I would put the pen down.

When the next writer's support group meeting took place I had little to show my friends. I read portions of the two pages of notes I had written:

> It's hard to imagine that anyone would deliberately kill her own baby. Once, when I read about child sacrifice in primitive cultures, an air of self-righteous indignation stirred within me. How could anyone take her own flesh and blood, the miracle of a newborn baby, and serve it up to some deity of stone or fire? Yet, today over 1.3 million babies are killed annually—sacrificed to the god of convenience.
>
> I didn't share the news of this pregnancy with anyone but my husband and the doctors who had confirmed my suspicions.
>
> My own beliefs corroded away; too frightened to lose my husband, I silently agreed to his terms. I'd have to walk this path alone.

I finished reading and put my head down, exhausted from the emotional tension. No one spoke for a few moments.

"Let's pray for Pat," Diane said softly. The compassion in her voice reassured me of her love.

My friends rose and gathered around me, each finding a place on my shoulders, my arms, to rest her hand. The loving touch of acceptance and their words to God poured over me like a balm, reaching down into the raw, ragged wounds.

Words of entreaty on my behalf began their cleansing cycle. "Dear Jesus, heal the hurts caused by this abortion. Guide Pat in the ways of discovery you have planned for her. Let her feel your love and forgiveness, Father." Tears flowed as each woman felt my pain in the way only another woman could. I was grateful.

"Pat, have you spoken to anyone at the Crisis Pregnancy Center?" asked Tamara.

"No."

"I think you might want to talk to the counselors there. They work with women who have had abortions as well as young women who are facing a crisis pregnancy. Why don't you call them? They may be able to direct you to some sort of support group."

Tamara's suggestion proved to be insightful. I never would have considered it on my own.

Early the next morning I dialed the center's number. After introducing myself to the pleasant voice on the phone, I explained the reason for my call.

The young woman said they had received other calls from women who—like me—had delayed reactions to an abortion that had taken place years before. She offered to arrange an appointment with the director of the center and I accepted.

My appointment was scheduled for 10:30, Thursday morning, at their San Jose office. When Thursday morning came, I felt apprehensive as I pulled into the center's

parking lot. The small office was tucked inconspicuously toward the back of a commercial center.

Opening the plate glass door I noticed that the waiting room looked like any other business lobby. A receptionist's desk sat to one side. A few chairs were neatly lined up against two side walls. The muted peach walls balanced a business gray carpet. Impressionist posters were mounted in simple brushed chrome frames and hung around the room.

A petite woman, smartly dressed in a two-piece pink linen suit greeted me with a warm smile and handshake.

"I'm Connie Davis, the director here." Her deep chestnut colored hair set off her gleaming hazel eyes. "Why don't you join me in my office?"

Family portraits on her neat desk, potted plants, and comfortable wingback chairs made the small room inviting and intimate.

Once she sat down at her desk, she asked, "How can I help you, Pat?"

"Eleven years ago I had an abortion." I didn't wait to see her reaction before I rattled on. "I was married to the father of my baby and he didn't want another child." I crossed my legs uncomfortably.

"I don't know what made me decide to have the abortion. Looking back on the situation, I can't imagine why I did such a thing. But at the time, I was afraid my husband would leave me. Eight months after my abortion he left anyway." I paused to a take a breath and looked Connie in the face for the first time.

Her eyes revealed a compassion I hadn't expected.

"First of all, Pat, it's important that you understand that what you just described was a crisis pregnancy." She paused a moment for me to absorb what she said.

She had piqued my curiosity. "What do you mean?"

"Your husband's response left you feeling confused, vulnerable, and alone. Forced to make a quick decision, you weren't able to think clearly because of your hormonal and emotional condition."

"I never considered the possiblity that my decision had been affected by my physical condition."

Connie continued, "In the first weeks of pregnancy our bodies go through radical physical changes. Large doses of hormones are released, which can make you susceptible to extreme mood swings. These emotional swings affect your ability to approach the decision rationally. What you would do today is probably quite different than what you decided when you discovered you were pregnant."

"No doubt about that!" I raised my eyebrows in agreement. "But Connie, I'm here today because of an extreme reaction I had the other evening. While watching a pro-life film I almost became hysterical from an inner pain that seemed to grip me. I don't know where that pain is coming from."

Connie shook her head as if she knew exactly what I was describing. "We're now seeing more and more cases just like yours, Pat."

"Really? I've been a Christian for 10 years. I know I'm forgiven. And I've seen other pro-life films, but they didn't bother me. Why did I suddenly have such an intense emotional reaction?"

"Apparently, you've had a delayed reaction to the traumatic experience of your abortion. Millions of women have had abortions since it was legalized 14 years ago. Many of them, who had their abortions five or ten years before, were forced, by the secrecy surrounding their abortion, to suppress their feelings. They are suddenly reacting years later just as you did the other night."

"You mean other women are having the same experience?"

"Pat, our offices are receiving phone calls every day from women suffering a variety of symptoms."

"Other symptoms?" I was intrigued by her comment. "What are some of them?"

"They're not unlike those we've seen in other victims of trauma." Connie stood up to move to the bookcase next to her. She reached over and handed me a small pamphlet as she continued. "Some women experience flashbacks to the events surrounding the decision, frequent bouts of depression, unexplained mood swings and unexplained outbursts. Others succumb to substance abuse, promiscuity. The brochure I handed you lists some of the symptoms."

I glanced at the pictures and some of the words, but my mind raced back over the past 11 years.

"I think I've experienced some of the symptoms you've mentioned. But what do I do next? I've discussed my abortion with my counselor, but he never connected it with some of the emotional problems I've been experiencing."

"Most counselors aren't aware of the correlation. As I said, we're just beginning to piece the puzzle together ourselves."

"Do you have a support group for post-abortion trauma— that is what you called it, right?"

"Unfortunately, at this time we don't, but we're planning to start one in the very near future. What we have noticed, however, is that there seems to be a need to experience the grief, to actually mourn the loss of your baby."

"You mean like the same mourning period for any loved one?"

"Something like that."

When I left Connie's office I sat in my car for a few minutes. I had no idea how to begin the long road that lay before me.

"Lord, please help me."

Once again I headed to the bookstore. A number of books discussed the abortion issue from a political or legal standpoint, a few dealt with the scriptural perspective. I found only one that described a woman's journey toward health after an abortion. Nevertheless, I bought them all.

Will I Cry Tomorrow? by Susan Stanford was an account of her struggle to heal the pain of her abortion. A psychologist, her expertise led her to seek understanding for the consequences she experienced in her life as a result of her abortion. She offered steps for the reader to take to heal the abortion memory.

Interestingly, she suggested gathering all the details and feelings surrounding the abortion. The suggestion of Ruth, my writer's support group friend, had been insightful.

Blessed are those who mourn, for they will be comforted. The familiar passage came rushing to my mind. As long as I denied my grief, God was unable to console me., but He wanted to pour out His compassion, to set me free from the inner pain I suppressed for so many years. Before he could do that, however, I would have to allow my grief to surface.

I returned to my journal and pressed through.

Long forgotten feelings and thoughts began to surface. Recounting the events leading to my abortion, I realized how fearful I had been that my marriage might end if I had another child. I discovered that my inability to communicate my true feelings misled my husband into believing an abortion was an acceptable alternative.

One morning I remembered a childhood vow long

forgotten in my memory—never to cry when I was hurt. That vow allowed me only one emotion to express my pain once the abortion had taken place—rage.

As I chronicled the events after my abortion I began to see the link between the inner rage at myself and my husband and our eventual divorce.

Unable to openly grieve the loss of my baby I turned my pain inward and began to anesthetize it by abusing alcohol.

I sought out books to help me understand the trauma I was experiencing. But I soon discovered there was very little information available on post-abortion recovery.

Next, I began to study books on grief to gain the insight I needed. I had experienced various levels of grief when I went through my divorce, when my parents died, when I had my heart attack, and even when I had to move from our townhome. I learned that the stages of grief were similar in every form of loss.

Instinctively, I allowed long suppressed responses of anger to rise to the surface. I faced the guilt and shame I had denied for so long. And I released the restrained tears of disappointment and sadness. Encouraged by the healing I was experiencing in my own life, I began to put together the rudimentary beginnings of a book proposal in hopes it would help other women.

I looked forward to my lunch with Diane. The Good Earth restaurant in Los Gatos was our favorite hangout. The natural foods restaurant with its overabundance of hanging plants, comfortable atmosphere, and fresh, healthy entrees helped us justify our three- and four-hour luncheons. Today I had a surprise and I couldn't wait to show her.

"Sorry I'm late."

"Oh, Pat, it's so good to see you," Diane gave me a warm smile. "What's this all about? You sounded so mys-

terious on the phone."

"Diane, I'm so excited. I wanted you to be the first one to know where I'm going."

"You're going somewhere?"

"I'm going to the Mount Hermon Writer's Conference."

"Oh Pat, that's great." She cupped her hands together and placed them over her mouth with obviously delight.

"But the twinkle in your eyes says there's something else you have up your sleeve," she said with a gleam in her own eyes.

I reached inside a large manila envelope and pulled out a folder.

"I've finished a book proposal on my abortion." I pushed the folder toward her on the table, "I wanted you to be the first to see it. You've been the one who's inspired me and kept me going these past few months."

"Oh Pat, how wonderful!" She put her fingers to her lips and tears welled up in her eyes. "I know all the pain this represents. You've moved past so much grief in the last five months."

Gently she passed her hand over the manuscript. I knew she would understand the deeper meaning of my announcement. And I was right.

"When will you be going?"

"The first of April. This is your copy, I want you to mark it up, point out any flaws. I'm really apprehensive about going," I confessed.

"You'll do just fine. I'll be praying for you, I know God has done a great deal for you already as you've prepared this proposal," she said patting the cover. "I'm sure He has much more in store for you."

I nodded in agreement. But I had little idea that day of the full meaning of Diane's remark.

INSIGHT QUESTIONS FOR CHAPTER 5

1. When abortion is mentioned in public, do you find yourself reacting physically, e.g. tightening your stomach muscles, clenching your teeth or holding your breath? Describe your physical reactions.

2. Describe ways in which you struggle to ignore feelings connected to your abortion(s). Have you told yourself over and over to forget about it?

3. How do you feel you need to disguise your reaction(s) when the subject of abortion is discussed?

4. Are you affected by physical reminders of your abortion? Are you uncomfortable around babies? Pregnant women? Children?

5. Are there certain times of the year when you find yourself depressed, sick or accident prone, such as the anniversary date of the abortion or the month of the would-be birth date of your baby?

6. Which of the following statements can you identify with and why?
    "It's only fetal tissue, it's not a baby."
    "Everyone told me I was doing the right thing."
    "When life begins has been debated for years; everyone has to decide for herself whether it begins at conception or birth."
    "Abortion is legal so how can it be wrong?"

6

...

Naked and
Ashamed

*. . . I was afraid because I was naked; and I hid
myself* (Gen 3:10).

The hairpin turn into the Mount Hermon campground in
the Santa Cruz Mountains cut through groves of giant
coastal redwoods. Ponderosa pine, big-leaf maple, and red
alder stood sentenial over lush green undergrowth that
carpeted the forest floor. Red huckleberry, sorrel, trillium,
and fairy lantern were about to explode into springtime
blossoms. Lacy sword fern sparkled from the sun glistening off the morning dew.

Winding down the two lane road, over a small bridge,
and into the parking lot outside the administration building, I wondered what the next few days held in store for

me. It's one thing to tell your friends you've had an abortion, I thought; it's another to share your truth with people you've never met. Dear God, help me have the courage I need.

After checking in, I drove my little blue Honda to a rustic cabin at the base of a hill, about a quarter of a mile from the main meeting area. The cool moist air was layered with the odor of pine and wet earth.

Only 15 miles from the Pacific Ocean, Mount Hermon sat in a cool, shaded area of a coniferous forest where the coastal fog rolled in most evenings and lingered until mid-morning. I trudged inside, lugging suitcases, pillow, bookbag, briefcase, plus a complete wardrobe on hangers.

It was the perfect setting for a fledging writer: twin beds covered in rust-colored chenille bedspreads, a small desk with a lattice-back chair and a gooseneck lamp, and two built-in wardrobe closets with a sink tucked between them.

Yes, it would do, I thought. The conference brochure listed an active schedule. Publishers, and editors from some of the largest Christian publishing houses and magazines would be there. My anxiety grew with each passing moment.

Would I be able to tell my story? Was I really a capable writer? What would Christians think about me once they knew my secret? Dear God, I hoped I knew what I was doing.

Dinner would be served at 5:30 p.m.

Any bravado I might have had on the drive up, slowly ebbed as I walked down the path to the dining commons. Childhood feelings of timidity stalked my mind, along with old feelings of inadequacy. For a moment I listened to the familiar taunts: *What makes you think you can write? These are real professionals. Writers.*

A cacophony of chattering voices rose from the 350 conferees already around the tables. Men casually dressed in sweaters, sport shirts, and jeans mingled and laughed with each other. Middle-aged women chatted amiably with younger women.

Feeling like a bit player in what I was certain was a sea of celebrities, I took the first open seat I could find at a large round table with seven others. A sign in the middle heralded the name of an editor who would host our meal. I learned later that mealtimes at Mount Hermon allowed the aspiring writer to meet informally with editors face-to-face.

I felt small and insignificant, yet conspicuous. My palms were sweaty, and my tongue felt dry; words clung to the roof of my mouth. It reminded me of my first day at school when everyone seemed to loom over me and I was convinced they understood some secret code of conduct I didn't.

"What type of writing are you interested in?" An older woman with a natural pink glow was looking directly at me, her crystal clear blue eyes twinkling under rimless glasses.

"I guess a personal testimony is the best way to describe it."

"Nonfiction then?"

Of course, dummy, that's what you should have called it. My inner heckler was having a great time.

"Yes, exactly." I tried to recoup from my display of ignorance.

"What's your topic?"

"Abortion recovery." I stared at my plate, and began to carve my meat with the precision of a brain surgeon.

"I see. How interesting." Without further comment she turned to the person on her left and repeated the same question.

"Are you a counselor?" A plump woman across from me asked.

"No, actually I'm an advertising consultant." I was grateful for the mask of my profession.

"Well then, what prompted you to write a book on abortion recovery?"

The moment of truth. I tried to steady my voice. "I had an abortion . . . *before* I was a Christian."

"Oh, uhuh." Her voice lowered along with her eyes. Awkwardly she continued eating.

Suddenly I felt naked and ashamed. I wanted to drop as inconspicuously as possible through the floor, so I turned my attention toward my meal. Eyes glued to the portions laid before me, I methodically consumed each one before moving to the next.

Head down, I listened intently to the conversations that swirled around me. Words such as queries, rejection slips, proposals, and clippings somersaulted across the table, as I began to learn the language of writing.

Over the years, I'd discovered each profession has its own means of communication, with a special vocabulary of terms that exposed newcomers. Writers, editors, and publishers were no exception.

Later, as I trudged back to my cabin after the meal, I questioned my own sanity for thinking I could traverse this new-found chasm of ignorance. The next day loomed in front of me like a dark rain cloud. Yet within its rolling nemesis there was a promise of fresh growth.

"Issues and Trends" read the schedule. The afternoon workshop was headed by a young editor from a prominent publishing house. During a discussion on the various topics that dominated the news, the subject of abortion came up.

"I'm a doctor at a major hospital in L.A.," began a

youthful male voice from the back of the room. "Practically every day, I see young women who are faced with an unwanted pregnancy. Just last week a 13-year-old, a child herself, came to the day clinic and requested an abortion."

When I turned to see who was talking, I discovered a young man hardly out of his twenties. Dressed in the intentional casualness of cashmere, he looked more like a fraternity pledge with freckles and slightly tousled reddish-brown hair.

"Although I'm a Christian, I don't mind admitting I signed the necessary papers." He crossed his legs, feet in woven leather loafers without sox. "How could I force her to live out a life sentence she was incapable of coping with?"

"Yes, that's a good point. We need to be open to different approaches to this issue. We can't assume there is only one answer to so complex a matter as this one." Our instructor's comment was brisk and assured.

I was shocked. It had never occurred to me that Christians would differ on the issue.

"I have a friend who was raped, and I know if she'd become pregnant she would have wanted to abort the baby," a middle-aged blonde near the front of the room joined in.

"I did have an abortion."

The words had simply floated out of my mouth.

"Sir, I know you probably thought you were giving that young girl a second chance by helping her have an abortion." I turned to face the young doctor. "But from my own experience, I know the pain she may now have to endure. I've just begun to face the consequences of my own actions."

A hush settled across the room like silt.

Beyond the Hidden Pain of Abortion

"I was raped," said a determined voice behind me.

Her self-disclosure filled the room with whispers of shifted papers and creaking chairs. I glanced around. Across the room, almost hidden from view, was a diminutive, dark haired woman with eyes so smoky they seemed opaque.

"And I, too, had an abortion. It devastated me and nearly destroyed my marriage and deeply wounded my family."

The woman continued speaking in her soft, yet emotionless, monotone. "This woman is right." She gestured toward me, but her eyes were on the young doctor's face. "You probably thought you did the young girl a favor, but you may have sentenced her to a lifetime of regret." Her eyes shifted, reached out, and grabbed hold of mine.

I stared back at her. *She knew.*

Our instructor's lips formed thin ridges of anxiety. "It's apparent we won't solve this debate in this workshop, but it's a good example of the types of issues editors must face in their publications," he said quickly. "Let's move on."

My own thoughts were diverted, scurrying around gathering questions that had pestered me for answers in the past few months. I couldn't wait to meet the woman behind me.

Once the session ended, I walked up to her. My five-foot-two frame seemed imposing next to her.

"I'm Kathy Adamson." Her voice cuddled me close. "I'd like to applaud your bravery."

"My bravery?" Her remark startled me.

"This is your first conference, isn't it?"

"Why yes, how did you know?"

"You seemed unsettled by Christians who approve of abortion."

"I am. I never thought a Christian doctor would advise a

young girl to have one." My incredulity pinched my voice into my native Michigan twang.

"Some doctors, Christian counselors and even pastors, advise girls to have an abortion with very little understanding of what they're prescribing."

Her eyes grew reflective and a twinge of pain darted across them. "Most women don't tell anyone they've had one, so professionals are just beginning to see the devastation it brings. I've been involved in post-abortion recovery for almost 10 years. I know the problems some women have to contend with."

"Are there that many women—Christian women—who've had an abortion?" I knew the statistics, but they were faceless numbers. "You know, you're the first one I've ever met."

Kathy's voice was firm. "No," she corrected me gently. "I'm just the first one who has ever admitted it to you." She spoke with authority and conviction and I liked her right off.

"I've got to go to another workshop now." She glanced at her watch. "But why don't we have lunch together tomorrow. We'll talk more then."

Walking into the afternoon sunshine, I breathed the fresh air deep into my lungs. A new awareness of the significance of this conference was emerging. I wasn't sure if I was a writer or not, but I knew there was a purpose for my being there.

Breakfast was served at eight o'clock each morning. Unaccustomed to eating that early I reveled in the opportunity to stay in bed, waiting until the last possible moment before I showered and got ready. Being away from the daily pressures of my business, a constantly ringing telephone, and a busy teenager allowed me time to reflect on the events that brought me here.

93

Beyond the Hidden Pain of Abortion

The past 10 years had plunged me into an almost unrelenting grieving cycle. One after the other, four life-changing events, spun me into various levels of grief almost without a break. My divorce, the death of both my parents, and my heart attack taught me the importance of acknowledging my woundedness, of submitting to grief's healing process by accepting the pain.

And now, somehow, my intuition told me God was about to heal a deeper wound lodged silently within my soul.

My pace slowed to a laborious crawl as I struggled up the path toward Birch Lodge for the morning writing lab. The steep grade had revealed my pitifully inept physical condition and I stopped to gasp fresh air into my strained lungs.

"Excuse me," a voice called out. Turning, I saw a woman move effortlessly up the hill. Dressed in jeans, a navy blue turtleneck, and a white windbreaker, she looked like one of those vibrant young women in the Eddie Bauer catalogue. With a few short strides she was alongside me.

A shy smile slipped across her face. "I was at your dining table the first evening we were here." Her dark hair was cropped so that it bounced when she walked.

Casually, I glanced at her name tag. "I'm sorry, Lori from Seattle. I was so insecure that night I was totally myopic. I don't think I really saw anyone."

Her quick laugh said she understood. "I overheard your conversation about the book you're writing on abortion. I wondered if we could meet for a few moments to discuss it."

"Sure, but I'm meeting someone for lunch."

"How about after lunch? We could meet by the dining hall on one of the benches outside the hospitality center." She turned and pointed toward a quiet sitting area underneath a small grove of redwoods across the street.

"Say around one-thirty or so?"

"Great, I'll see you then."

With our appointment confirmed, she continued her agile climb up the hill. I huffed and puffed my way behind her, pledging with every inhale to sign up for an exercise course when I returned home.

Just before noon, I approached the bench where Kathy Adamson and I were to meet.

"Pat, over here." She waved. "I've been thinking alot about yesterday. I've got so many questions I want to ask you."

"Great, fire away." I sank down gratefully beside her and took in the garden view framed by a magnificent grove of redwoods.

"But first, tell me a little about yourself," I began. "I'd like to know what you do, and how know so much about women who have had abortions."

Kathy shifted slightly so she could see my face. "Until recently I belonged to WEBA, Women Exploited by Abortion. I've led a support group in my home for a number of years. But tell me why you're here, Pat?"

"About five months ago, I had an unexpected reaction to a pro-life video." As I poured out my story, she listened attentively.

"When my grief surfaced, I looked for books to help explain what was happening to me. I was surprised to find just a few, and only two had any material which dealt with the grieving process. So I decided to write one myself."

Kathy smiled. "Did you bring the manuscript to the conference?"

"It isn't written yet, but I did bring a proposal."

"Well, that's a start."

"Kathy, why do you think it took 11 years before my reaction began to surface for me?"

Beyond the Hidden Pain of Abortion

"Usually it's triggered by another grievous event: a death in the family, a job loss, or even the loss of a pet can be the pressure point God uses to start the mourning process. Had anything like that happened to you?"

"Why yes, I had a heart attack in 1985 and my mother died the next year." Pieces of the puzzle were clicking into place.

"You probably know from the research you've done, there are basically four or five steps in the grieving process. We move through each one in kind of a random order. Going from anger to depression, to bargaining, back to anger."

She paused to reflect. "Once a similar trauma occurs, it's as if an emotional plug is pulled. When we learn to accept each stage of grief, embrace it, allow ourselves to feel the pain, then we're able to come to a point of reconciliation, of forgiveness, and finally acceptance."

I nodded in recognition. "During the past five months I've worked through the anger stage and have had bouts of depression, but I'm not sure if I've come to a place of forgiveness, especially toward myself."

My face was a question mark waiting for a mentor's guidance.

"That's probably the hardest stage for all of us to move past, Pat. I really want to encourage you to come to some of our meetings." Gently she placed her hand on mine. "I have a new group starting. If you wouldn't mind driving to Redwood City, you could join us."

Kathy reached for her notebook and jotted down my name and address. "About seven or eight women, most of them Christians, meet once a week for about six weeks to discuss their abortion and how it has affected them. I'll send you some information and a notice about our next meeting."

"Please do. I'd really like to come." My resolve was set, I would join her support group.

Just then, a woman who had been in the afternoon workshop the day before approached us.

"A few of us were very moved by both of your stories yesterday and were wondering if you would hostess a special table at dinner. We'd like to invite those interested in knowing more about abortion from a personal perspective to join you."

Kathy's eyes met mine for an instant. "Sure," we answered simultaneously.

After lunch I meandered through the gardens toward the hospitality center reflecting on my conversation with Kathy. A breathtaking display was beginning to unveil itself. Spreading rhododendrons with their large, rose-purple clusters and two showy Pacific dogwood trees with tiny, first buds were preparing us for their spring blossoms.

The sun, breaking through the tops of the massive redwoods, cast a welcome warmth on my exhausted body.

"Feels good, don't you think?" Lori asked as she sat down beside me on the bench.

"It's wonderful. This is probably one of my favorite spots at Mount Hermon. It's so tranquil here. I love watching everyone walk by."

We sat quietly together as other conferees headed toward afternoon appointments with editors or scurried to get to another workshop on time.

"Pat, I wanted to talk to you because. . . ." She hesitated a second. "Fifteen years ago my husband Roger and I were living together, engrossed in the hippie life style. We didn't live too far from here, as a matter of fact; we'd often park our beat-up old Volkswagen van down at the beach in Santa Cruz."

97

Beyond the Hidden Pain of Abortion

It was difficult for me to envision the woman sitting next to me as a hip-hugging, bell-bottomed hippie. Her warm brown eyes sparkled when she smiled and her shy demeanor belied my image of a '70s flower child. Staring straight ahead, she hesitated as she selected her words carefully before she released them.

"We weren't married then. I got pregnant and we decided I should have an abortion."

Tears surfaced and she waited quietly as she handed me a sanctioned piece of herself. "I haven't shared that fact with anyone before." She tilted her head back and closed her eyes. "Up to now only Roger and I knew about it."

What once had been a secret secluded in her heart now lay bare. Her face turned toward me once again.

I nodded slowly, a tight knot rising in my throat. Minutes passed as I waited for her to continue. The sting of her confession held me captive.

"I know now, Pat, I don't want to hide the truth any more." She put her head down and studied her hands. Her voice grew stronger, "Roger and I moved to Seattle six years ago. He's become a pastor, and we have two teenage sons. Our lives have moved on. But a part of me has been missing all these years." The tears dropped silently on her lap. "And I need to find it again."

I rested my hand on her arm. We sat there, without words, grieving the loss of part of ourselves, as well as our babies. "Lori, this may sound trite, but thank you for telling me. Until I came to this conference, I'd never met another woman who'd had an abortion. I want you to know I understand. A part of me has been missing too."

"Roger and I have supported the pro-life efforts in our church, but I don't want to cower in shame any longer." Her voice grew stronger. "I want to tell someone what happened to me, how I feel on the day that would have

been my baby's birthday. How Roger and I have cried over what we've done—the regret, the loss, the pain. I know I'm forgiven, but it doesn't bring my baby back to me."

The next day, heading toward my cabin after my final workshop, I took a moment to rest in Central Hall. I sat down on one of the couches in front of the stone fireplace and leaned my head back. It hadn't begun to register fully yet, but I knew God had placed me in this setting for more than one purpose: In one day I had met two women with abortion experiences after a decade of silence.

Sunrays spilled through the windowpanes and pooled on the wood floor beneath my feet. Shifting my mind into neutral, I allowed the tension to slide out of my body.

"Would you mind if I join you?" asked a voice almost in a whisper.

I opened my eyes. A petite woman, around 50, peered down at me. "I hope I'm not disturbing you," she said meekly.

"Not at all." I placed my bag on the floor and slid to one side of the couch to give her room to sit beside me.

"I was in the workshop the other day when you spoke up. I want to tell you how much I appreciated your honesty. After hearing what you said, I thought maybe you could help me." She moved her face closer. "I haven't told this to anyone, but my daughter recently confessed she had an abortion a few years ago."

She waited a moment to watch my reaction. Her distress etched deep lines across her forehead. "I've been grieving ever since." The tears she fought to control spilled out the sides of her eyelids. Then the words pressed past her lips. "That baby would have been my first grandchild."

I sat quietly waiting for her to continue, but inside I was

shocked at hearing yet another confession of grief unexpressed because of an abortion.

"Apparently it happened when she was in college, away from home, before she married," the woman continued in a quiet voice. "She got pregnant and didn't want to hurt or embarrass us, so she had an abortion."

"Sometimes, our children are too ashamed to come to us when they're in trouble," I answered. "They're afraid they've let us down."

"That's exactly what she said." The woman sat up for a moment, then slumped back down as she spoke, almost to herself. "I understand it with my mind, but my heart can't seem to deal with the fact that I'll never hold my first grandchild."

Her words pierced my own emotional barricade and wandered into unexplored territory.

"I've looked forward to having grandchildren. Now, she's having trouble getting pregnant. That's why she told me about the abortion. I haven't told anyone else about this, not even her father. He would be so disappointed. You're the first person to know."

It had never occurred to me that others also would be wounded by one individual's decision to have an abortion. I had been so indoctrinated with the concept that abortion was a woman's private choice, a right to do what she wanted with her own body, that I was astonished by this woman's pain.

She was grieving—aching for a lost grandchild. She needed to mourn her own loss, to receive the support and comfort of her husband and close friends. Yet, she didn't want to hurt her daughter by exposing her secret. She, too, was forced to suffer in silence.

"Do you think I'll ever get over it?"

In actuality, I didn't know the answer to her question.

"I'm sure right now you're in a state of shock. You've just learned about it."

"And I don't want to condemn her," she interjected quickly.

"I'm sure you don't, but it still hurts."

"Oh yes, I'm surprised how much it does hurt." For several seconds she looked down at the crumpled hankie in her hands before she spoke. "You know, I haven't paid much attention to this whole abortion issue. I never thought it would touch my life." As she looked up, her eyes were pleading for help, "We've been Christians ever since we were married. My daughter was raised in the church. I still can't believe it happened."

"You musn't blame yourself," I said quietly. "I've just begun to deal with my own decision. And I've discovered I don't understand yet why I did what I did."

"How do I get past this?" Her words tumbled out now. "My heart is so broken, I find myself crying during the day—you know, when I'm alone. Even during my prayer time, I just weep and weep." Her shoulders slumped as if she carried a huge weight.

I sighed with understanding. "I don't know how long it will take, but one thing I have learned—it's important to have a time for mourning. God tells us, 'Blessed are those who mourn for they shall be comforted.' He wants us to grieve, to cry, to acknowledge our inner pain. It's then that He comes to comfort us."

"Do you really think it will ever be possible for me to forget this whole thing?"

"No, probably not. But the deep grief you're feeling now will subside. I suppose we'll sorrow forever. It's part of recognizing our loss. Periodically, you'll probably find yourself having a quick cry, but you'll move on." I reached over and placed one arm around her shoulder. "Why don't

we take a moment to pray together?"

"I'd like that very much." She squeezed my hand impulsively, "I'm so glad I told you."

We held hands and closed our eyes.

"Dear Father, you know my friend's pain, You've been with her when she's wept before You over the loss of her first grandchild." I could hear her take deep breaths, and large drops of tears spattered across our hands as she released her inner sorrow.

"Father comfort her, wrap Your arms around her, let her feel Your love for her, and her daughter. We ask now that You open her heart to receive the balm of Your Holy Spirit, our Comforter. Give her the wisdom she will need as she supports her daughter through these difficult days. And, Father, once her healing is complete, I pray You will bring others to her whom she can comfort. In Your precious Son, Jesus' name, Amen."

We sat for a few moments letting the sun wrap us in a quilt of warmth. I held her hand in mine as she regained her composure.

"Thank you for sharing your life with me, for trusting me with something so private." I looked into her eyes as she stood to leave. We smiled at one another, then I stood up. As we held each other for a moment, both of us knew we would probably never see each other again. Silently, she gathered her belongings and walked away.

It had been a brief encounter, yet one of deep intimacy for both of us; I felt God had bonded us together as women in a unique way.

Dinner began promptly at 5:30. I made my way around the hall trying to locate the table that had been set up for Kathy and me.

ABORTION. The card at the table had already attracted

a group of people, two men and four women. As we settled into our chairs, Lt. Colonel Henry Gariepy, editor of the Salvation Army's publications, opened the conversation.

"We're very interested in publishing a personal account article on abortion. Have either of you written one?"

"I've written several." Kathy remained poised.

"Well, I would like to see anything you'd like to submit, and you too, Pat." He smiled at me. "Of course, because of the type of ministry we are involved in, many of our readers are women who probably have had an abortion, and we need to know how to minister to them."

The colonel might have been shocked to discover how many of *those women* were seated close to him at the conference.

"Just being open to the fact that they have emotional pain connected with their ordeal is the first step," I said. "I know I feel guilty admitting I'm suffering from my decision," I added. "After all, I brought the pain upon myself. Although I'm embarrassed to say it, I'm suffering from a post-abortion reaction."

"Now what's that?" asked the colonel.

"It's similar to the type of post-trauma reaction we've seen in Vietnam veterans." Kathy's expertise was helping me handle my uneasiness.

"Would you mind elaborating on that?" The colonel put his fork down to absorb Kathy's explanation.

"Because the Vietnam war was so controversial, veterans were unable to express their pain or share their experiences openly. Instead, they were made to feel ashamed of their participation and were forced to hide their emotional wounds. Women who find themselves regretting their abortions feel the same type of inhibition."

"I'm beginning to get the picture." He nodded at the illustration Kathy used that he could relate to. "How many

103

women would you say experience post-abortion trauma?"

"They estimate 90 percent who have had an abortion have some type of emotional reaction. Probably 200,000 women a year need to seek counseling because of it."

"Wow!" The colonel sat back in his chair. "I had no idea the problems were so widespread." Slowly, he nodded his head, "I can see there's quite a need to let women know there are other women having similar experiences."

As he reached into his pocket and handed Kathy and me each his business card, he repeated, "I'm very interested in seeing an article from either of you."

Carole Gift Page, a prolific author who was leading one of the writing labs at the conference, listened intently. Finally she turned to me. "Pat, would you mind meeting me tomorrow in the auditorium after labs? I'd like to ask you some questions."

I had no idea why Carole wanted to speak to me, but it would turn out to have a significant impact on my life.

Built around 1915, the old wooden auditorium was a favorite landmark of the conference center. Floors creaked when you walked down its wide aisles. Curved, open beams exposed the building's skeleton, and expansive windows traversed the two side walls creating a marriage between the plushness of nature and the honest simplicity inside.

I walked through the sliding glass doors in the back just as Carole finished her morning lab. Inundated by a throng of aspiring writers, she slowly made her way to the back of the room. She joined me in one of the pews and kicked off her shoes.

"It's my feet that hurt the most." She smiled ruefully, wiggling her toes and rubbing the back of her neck.

Her large blue eyes were cordial and empathetic as she began, "I wondered if you could you tell me why you

decided to have an abortion, that's if you feel comfortable doing so."

Her voice indicated her genuine interest in me, not just for curiosity's sake, but because of a profound need to know, to understand why such a decision would be made.

I explained how it was like most crisis decisions, how my emotions had prevented me from thinking clearly. She listened compassionately until I was through.

Then she began slowly, "I lost a child at birth about six years ago." Her eyes glistened. "She was born with hydrocephalus. That's where fluid accumulates around the brain and prohibits it from developing properly. I knew when I was six months along in my pregnancy that my baby would be born abnormally." She paused to look out past the windows into the green lushness of the forest.

"The doctors suggested an abortion, but I refused. Abortion was never a consideration for me, so I've always wondered what would compel a woman to make such a decision."

Her gentle manner allowed me to be honest. "When I was confronted with my husband's resistance to a new baby, the truth is, Carole, I simply chose what seemed to be the easiest answer to my dilemma.

"Since then, I've learned many women have inital sporadic bleeding in the early stages of pregnancy, yet they deliver a healthy baby. If I were confronted with the same situation today I would do everything in my power to try to sustain my pregnancy."

"Pat, I was drawn to you yesterday because you revealed your need to grieve, but you said you felt guilty even expressing your pain. I lost a child, but I could grieve openly. Some people can't understand why a mother would grieve over an infant she hadn't even seen."

She reached into her totebag and handed me a pink

105

covered paperback. "It took me almost five years after I wrote about my experience to get this book published, and I'd like to give you a copy."

I read the title, *Misty, Our Momentary Child*, as Carole continued. "I approached every publisher I knew; I was compelled to keep pressing. Crossway books finally agreed to do it." As she rose to leave, she whispered, "I hope it will help you."

I thanked her for her thoughtfulness. But there was no way I could have understood then the tremendous gift Carole Page was giving me.

INSIGHT QUESTIONS FOR CHAPTER 6

1. Do you feel guilty for having had an abortion(s)? If so, why?

2. In what ways do you try to cover up for feelings of guilt?

3. Did you hide your abortion from anyone? If so, why?

4. Would you want to tell those individuals about your abortion now? If so, what would you tell them?

5. Are there aspects of your abortion that still make you feel ashamed?

6. What do you think would help relieve your feelings of guilt?

7
· · ·

No One
to Sit Shiva

Therefore, when Jesus saw her weeping, and the Jews who came with her weeping, He groaned in the spirit and was troubled . . . Jesus wept (John 11:33, 35)

"Sitting shiva," is an old Jewish custom of gathering together when a loved one dies, to sit with the bereaved and comfort them in their sorrow. However, no one comes to comfort those of us who grieve our babies from abortion, no one offers words of encouragement or prayers on our behalf, no one sends a card of sympathy.

We grieve alone.

"Yo, Mom, you're back! Unlocking the door to my apartment, I was almost bowled over by my son, backpack slung over his shoulder, munching on a raw hot dog with a slice of cheese and bologna wrapped around it.

"The phone's been ringing constantly while you've been gone." His mouth worked bits of cheese into his cheeks as he rattled off a litany of messages: "Prometheus Development called. They want to know if they can still make changes on this month's newsletter. Lincoln Property wants to delay their project by a week.

"Gotta go," he yelled as he charged out the door. "I've got a class in 20 minutes." A sophomore at San Jose State University, Kelly seemed to move, talk, and eat perpetually.

"Hey, Sissy, when did you get back?" My sister walked toward me from the living room, her open arms and bright smile a welcome greeting. The youngest of my three sisters and 14 years my junior, Lorraine had lived with me since she was 18. Now in her late 20s, she was my best friend. Kelly, Lorraine, and I shared the small, two bedroom, two bath apartment down the street from our old townhome.

"How'd it go? Was anyone interested in your book?" she asked excitedly. My sister had watched me struggle to finish my proposal before the conference.

"You're not going to believe this, but I didn't submit my proposal," I admitted as I dropped my briefcase to the floor. "I was too intimidated."

"Seriously? You didn't show it to anyone?" Her question was punctuated by a look of astonishment, complete with raised eyebrows and Betty Boop eyes.

"You crack me up," she said stuffing her hands into her jeans pockets. "You're always challenging Kelly and me to not be afraid, to go for it, take a risk. Now you're telling me you spent all that time preparing a proposal, not to

mention all that money on a writer's conference and then never. . . ."

She threw her head back and laughed out loud, delighted by her big sister's bout with the jitters. Her auburn hair glistened from the sun streaming through the dining room window. She shook her index finger in mock rebuke.

"I know, I know." I held up both hands in a gesture of surrender. "But so many things happened, I can't wait to tell you."

We let the morning slide into afternoon like grease on a hot griddle as we talked and sipped coffee.

"Lor, I can't believe all the incredible chance encounters I had with women who've had an abortion experience. I know it's part of my healing somehow."

My sister's face grew serious. "You know, Pat, you can't continue to be involved in this whole recovery process without telling your son. You're going to have to tell Kelly about your abortion."

Lorraine was the only family member who knew my secret. She paused to let the idea take hold in my mind. "You wouldn't want him to hear it from someone else."

"Lorraine, I have to be honest. I'm scared. Kelly and I have been through so much."

My mind scanned the personal disappointment, physical and financial hardships, career and life style changes we'd endured the past 12 years. I paused to weigh the cost of self-disclosure: my fear of losing him was the real issue.

"It's been buried for so long. Let's face it, I've lied to him by committing the sin of omission. I'm not sure how he'll respond. What will he think of me?"

I valued Lorraine's spiritual maturity. "God will give you the courage to be honest with Kelly and He'll help him understand and accept you."

I knew my sister spoke the truth. "Remember, Sissy, we've all missed the mark, just 'sinners saved by grace.' Hey, that's what being a Christian is all about, right?"

A Bible school graduate, Lorraine's spiritual growth, stemming from a sincere desire to follow her convictions in the face of personal sacrifice and adversity, helped me grow, too. I trusted her. We had been through difficult times together, yet, those very experiences enabled us to grow closer and deepen our relationship.

But mustering courage for this disclosure was another matter. I continued lamely, "Our lives are finally starting to settle down, Kelly's doing well in college, my business is growing, I'm just coming to grips with this whole ordeal myself."

She waited a moment, choosing her words carefully. "Trust the Jesus in him, Pat. Kelly loves you, and he loves the Lord. He'll get through this, and he'll be a better man for it, too."

I was aware of the deep emotional wound my divorce had inflicted on Kelly. In our moments together I tried to soothe the embedded pain with love, laughter, and emotional support. My new consulting business allowed me to work at home, to be there for him in a way I'd hadn't in the past.

When the semester began that fall, I noticed he started coming home between classes, so we could "hang out" together, as he put it. He decided to live at home because he felt we needed to reconnect after he'd lived with his dad for a year while I recovered from my heart attack.

"I know you're right, but meeting Kathy Adamson at the writer's conference showed me how much healing I still need to experience; there's much more to this recovery process than I was aware of." I rubbed my forehead trying to ease the tension I felt rising inside. "Besides, I

don't think I've fully mourned my baby."

My sister's eyes grew pensive. Then I noticed her tears. "Every time we discuss this whole abortion situation, I'm surprised by my reaction. I feel such a loss, I can't help wondering what she would have been like."

"You've never shared that with me before." My own eyes burned from the sting of tears in response.

"I think I felt like I'd cause you more pain. But ever since you told me, I've had to work through my own grief." Her lips quivered, her voice grew soft, wistful. "I have a little niece I didn't have a chance to meet."

"We'll see her someday, Sissy," I whispered.

"I know, I know. Please forgive me if I've made you sad," she said reaching across the table to stroke my hand. "I do love you, Pat."

"I know you do. I never thought my actions would hurt you, too. I'm sorry, Lor, please forgive me?"

Her hand squeezed mine as she slowly nodded her head.

Turning my head away from the hurt in her eyes, I finally said, "It's a fact of my life. I have to face the truth of it, Lor." I didn't know how prophetic those words would be.

Overwhelmed with experiences at the writer's conference, I needed time to recoup, to sort out the myriad encounters I'd had. Finally, with my business responsibilities under temporary control and a clear appointment book for the day, I decided to lounge around in my robe and read Carole's book.

Catalogs, notes, handouts from the conference, pieces of paper with names and telephone numbers were strewn around my work area. Finally, I found the pink paperback, *Misty Our Momentary Child.*

When God confronted me on the first page of the book,

I asked myself, "Pat, are you ready to face the full pain of your abortion?" Hesitantly, I answered yes, as I pushed on through the pages.

As Carole's story unfolded, I learned she had used an intrauterine device as a method of birth control for 10 years before reading in a magazine article that an IUD could cause an abortion by acting *after* the egg is fertilized, thus preventing implantation on the uterus wall. When she became aware of how the IUD functioned, she knew instantly it was no longer an acceptable means of birth control for her.

Abortion was abhorrent to her. My appreciation for her grew as I realized she had never indicated anything but acceptance of me as a person although she must have been repulsed by my sin.

With the birth of their second child, Carole and her husband Bill discovered an ABO blood incompatibility, similar to the Rh factor, which could threaten future children. Besides, pregnancy carried added risks for a woman over 35.

Yet, here was a woman so committed to the principles of God, she was willing to jeopardize her own well-being rather than terminate her pregnancy through abortion. In the face of medical logic, she followed her godly convictions.

And there I was, so committed to my own selfish fears and desires that I had quickly decided to snuff out my child's flame of life in the name of convenience.

I was caught up in Carole's experience. As she wrote of the events leading up to the birth of her daughter and the few hours of Misty's life, I was aware of how her faith in God sustained her, how her belief in a Creator's purpose, which allowed her to submit to God's unusual request of her, to believe for and then bear a child He would take to

be with Him so quickly.

Her faith and trust stirred me. My own response to my unexpected pregnancy stood naked in contrast to hers:

Haughty. Prideful.

Arrogant in my self-determination, I had rejected the reality of a Creator-God, an infinite God, an all-knowing God. My own audacity never allowed me to consider the possibility of a purpose beyond my own limited under-standing. And now, as I read Carole's book, I realized my daughter, her life stilled in a few short weeks, had a purpose for being in God's plan. But my self-importance had thwarted it.

The grief I felt was overwhelming. As the curtains of self-revelation parted, torrents of tears burst from inside me as I faced the enormous reality hidden from my sight.

Time and time again I lay the book aside to weep. At other times, unable to stop reading for hours, I continued my own journey through sorrow.

> I was holding her and taking her picture in the other room, Bill tells me. He snaps a couple of shots of me holding her. Then we both talk to her and kiss her. We assure her that "Mommy and Daddy love you and Jesus loves you too. . . ."[1]

I recalled the excitement that surrounded the birth of Kelly. How his father had walked around the hospital nursery with three cameras hanging from his neck; a Polaroid, a 35 millimeter, and a movie camera. He grinned from ear to ear with delight. Yet, our daughter had not delighted her daddy and her mommy had rejected her; both of us had withheld our love from her. My cries were inconsolable.

Grief gripped me. I wanted my mother to hold me, to

113

grieve with me. My daughter is dead. My daughter is dead, I screamed in my head. Someone please hold me, rock me, comfort me. I pulled at my clothing, I wanted to rip my heart out, the pain was so great.

Carole's insight became my own:

As I lie in bed reflecting over the day's events, two important insights gradually take shape in my mind. First, I've discovered that in a time of loss and grief, it takes a while for your emotions to catch up with your head knowledge. What's more, you can't escape feeling the pain. It will catch up with you sooner or later, and I'm beginning to realize the pain is necessary for the healing.[2]

The excruciating pain I was experiencing was part of my healing. Sobs, groans, tears, the very wrenching of my soul were all part of the mending process. I lay in bed trying to grapple with the truth.

The darkness of evening tiptoed in when I heard a key in the lock at the front door.

"Sissy, are you home?" Lorraine called out.

"I'm in the bedroom, Lor."

After a few moments Lorraine opened our bedroom door and flicked on the light. "Why are you lying in the dark? Are you sick?" she asked with concern in her voice.

"Just decided to take a day off, you know, a 'being' day," I lied. I wasn't ready to share my thoughts and feelings with anyone yet. Pulling myself out of bed, I stuffed my pain back inside.

"What shall we have for dinner?"

That night I awoke with a jolt. My hair and my night-gown damp with perspiration told me the dream was

shockingly real. Its horror lingered in my mind. "I hate you, I hate you," I had screamed as I jabbed the knife deep into my belly. Over and over again the blade disappeared into my flesh.

Why did I do it, kill my own baby? Oh my God, I said it, I killed my baby!

I fought with the blackness of the night. *Jesus, I've got to trust You. Your Word says I'm forgiven. Please, dear Jesus, let it be true.*

The morning light crept across the wall of my bedroom. My eyelids opened, but I lay still. I would feign sleep while Lorraine and Kelly clattered around the kitchen preparing for their day. The drone of the hair dryer in the bathroom lulled me into a mental no man's land. Behind me lay the devastation of yesterday's truths, ahead of me lay a battle with the unknown.

Dear Jesus, how many other women lie awake grieving their lost children? How many are tormented by questions of why, why, why? How many hide in their shame, too afraid to admit their pain, to seek comfort because their shame would be exposed?

I heard the front door shut. I waited a few minutes until I heard Lorraine's car drive off. Then I arose to go into the bathroom. I glanced in the mirror.

How could I have allowed myself to block out so much of who I am? But who am I? I thought I knew me, but who are you? The woman I faced in the mirror that morning was a stranger.

The warm mist slithered over the top of the shower door clouding the mirror in front of me. "For now we see in a mirror, dimly, but then face to face. Now I know in part, but then I shall know just as I also am known" (1 Cor. 13:12). The once favorite passage from the book of First

Corinthians left a haunting sense of dread at the prospect of knowing the full truth of what I'd done.

Dear Jesus, Your Word says You're the only one who knows me fully. Help me understand what's happening to me. I stepped into the hot water, put my head down in its pulsating spray.

I returned to bed, determined to finish Carole's book, and hopefully to bring closure to my own journey of mourning.

> Tuesday, January 12, the funeral.
> We stop in a section of the cemetery where only infants are buried. . .
> A spray of tiny pink roses, pink and white carnations and daisies grace the little coffin. Surrounding it are beautiful bouquets and vases of flowers . . . we are not gathered just to mourn a death but to celebrate life as well.[3]

I could hardly continue. "My sweet daughter, where did they lay you to rest?" I moaned.

> Everyone files by to greet us, give us a warm embrace, tell us they love us. Many have tears in their eyes.[4]

My heart broke as I realized I wanted others to love my daughter. But warm embraces would not encircle me. I mourned my baby alone.

Then an entry in Carole's journal caught me off guard.

> Friday, May 28: The newspapers are filled with articles about the seventeen thousand aborted fetuses found in a large steel cargo container.

I can't stop thinking about the women, those seventeen thousand mothers who allowed someone to rip out their offspring, flesh of their flesh, those tender miracles-tiny, precious, unkept promises. Are we so vastly different that those mothers could cast away like trash what I strived so desperately to save? What has happened to the mother-hearts? Have they all been stilled, anesthetized?[5]

My sobs became laments. Hours passed. I could not stop crying.

I wonder. Have these women who forfeited their babies ever glimpsed the miracle? Do they know anything of loss? Do they grieve secretly in the dead silence of night? Does it ever come back to haunt them—the specter of a child who was and then was not? Do they have any idea what they've done?[6]

My tears had turned into hysteria. I wrapped my arms across my chest and rocked back and forth. "You'll be all okay, you'll be okay," I sang over and over.

Finally, in desperation, I phoned my friend, Janice. Janice had held my hand and prayed for me in the ICU unit after they told me I was having a heart attack. She wrapped her arms around me at the foot of my mother's death bed. She wiped the tears from my face as I confessed spiritual failures and prayed prayers of forgiveness and healing for me. Now I needed the warmth of her voice to console me once again.

"What's wrong? What's happened?" she asked anxiously.

"I can't stop crying," I gasped. "It's about my abortion. Please pray for me."

"I'm holding you," she said, instinctively lowering her

voice to a mother's gentle soothing. Without asking any questions she began to pray.

"Dear Jesus." It was as if she were a small child whispering to her all-powerful Daddy. "Please, come and wrap Your arms around my friend. You alone know her pain, and You alone can heal the ache in Pat's heart." She paused to allow her words to penetrate my despondency. "Jesus, I can only stand with her in my love as her friend, but You, heavenly Father, can remove the sting. You can soothe the raw wound with the balm of Your love. Come now, dear Jesus, and heal my friend."

The warmth of Jesus' presence filled the room. I could feel His arms around me. My sorrow became His. He had come to bring His sweetness to comfort my bitterness. Peace settled about me like a billowing canopy. The racing thoughts stilled. My heartbeat slowed down.

"I love you, friend," Janice murmured softly. We sat silently for a few moments, as she allowed her simple presence at the other end of the phone to embrace me. She was Jesus' voice, speaking words of support, a woman, a mother, who could only imagine my heartbreak. I felt loved.

"Do you want to talk about what's happened?" she asked gently.

"I'm not sure I can." My breathing was still labored. "I know Jesus is leading me through a process of healing." Janice was one of the few friends in whom I had confided my secret.

I took deep breaths, filling my lungs to their capacity, then slowly exhaling. I could feel my composure returning. "Your prayers have brought me solace. Thank you, friend."

I stayed in bed three more days. I ached and mourned, sighed and yearned, cried and felt the fullness of my bereavement.

My family moved cautiously around me, sensing my need for isolation. Yet I wasn't alone. Jesus *sat shiva* beside me, My grief His, His grief mine.

Still, I wasn't ready to face daily life yet. Somewhere deep inside I perceived a need to allow the grief to continue without interruption.

One morning, as I slipped into the kitchen to brew a cup of coffee, I glanced over at the calendar hanging on the wall.

In four months I'll be 44.

Then it hit. *I'll never birth a baby again.*

My mind raced to scene after scene of my daughter's life: a crawling infant, a toddler taking her first steps, the white eyelet baby bonnets, the black patent leather Mary Janes, the lace trimmed anklets, the mother/daughter teas, her wedding day that would never be.

I was lost in grief again, swimming in a sea dark with waves of all that had been forfeited, destroyed.

Finally on the fifth day, Lorraine entered the veil I had placed around myself.

"Pat, we need to talk. Kelly is concerned. He knows you're depressed and he's frightened. You haven't gotten dressed for almost a week. I know you're mourning, but he doesn't understand what's happening to you." My sister was having difficulty holding in her concern. "I know you're trying, but you need to at least attempt to explain what's going on to him."

"You're right," I answered, "but the tears just don't stop."

"I understand, Pat, but eventually there comes a time to rise up and go on." She sat at the foot of my bed, opened her Bible and began to read.

To everything there is a season,

119

A time for every purpose under the heaven;
A time to be born, and a time to die,
A time to plant, and a time to pluck what is planted;,
A time to kill, and a time to heal,
A time to break down, and a time to build up;
A time to weep, and a time to laugh,
A time to mourn, and a time to dance (Eccles. 3:1-4).

"Sissy, I think its time for you to wash up and start to live again," she said softly as she looked at me with eyes of compassion. I sat enveloped in my sweet sister's gentleness.

"At least have dinner with us tonight," she said as she patted my feet and raised herself off the bed. "Then think about how you're going to tell Kelly, I think the time has come."

I nodded. Yes, the time had come. The thought of telling my son of my hidden shame brought a wave of nausea over me. Yet, I knew God was asking me to yield to His provision.

INSIGHT QUESTIONS FOR CHAPTER 7

1. What were some of the ways you mourned the loss of your baby at the time of your abortion?

2. Are there any particular thoughts or feelings that repeatedly plague you in regard to your abortion experience?

3. Unrelieved anxiety may lead to feelings of grief. Grief is often accompanied by great physical or mental

pain. If you've experience such pain, try to write a description or draw a picture that depicts how you felt.

4. Tears may be an expression of your feelings of grief. King David wrote, "I am weary with my groaning; all night I make my bed swim; I drench my couch with tears (Psalm 6:6). What are some of the ways you've expressed your grief?

5. What other ways of expression would help you ease the pain you felt or still feel? God promises to wipe away the tears from the faces of all his people. Before continuing, insert your name into the following sentence: God will personally wipe away all of _____ tears from her face.

8
...

Tears Are
a Special Grace

*Confess your trespasses to one another, and pray
for one another, that you may be healed* (James 5:16).

For days I agonized and prayed for God's wisdom. The
time had arrived to face Kelly and tell him about my
abortion.

My healing process had begun and part of that process
included trusting the relationship Kelly and I shared. I had
to believe it could endure the pressure the truth would
place on it.

But the knot in my stomach when I awoke that morning
warned of the risk I would be taking. What would it cost
our relationship when he heard I'd not only had an abortion, but I'd hidden it from him?

Beyond the Hidden Pain of Abortion

I headed out of my bedroom and into the kitchen. Coffee. Its strong acidic odor, richly brewed, circled through the room. "Kelly, when will you be back from your morning classes?"

"Around 11 o'clock, why?" he said as he carefully slurped hot coffee from a huge ceramic mug he had appropriated as his personal property. He leaned against the counter letting the steam rise to warm his face.

"I wanted to discuss something with you. How about if I have some sausage and potatoes ready when you get back?"

"Sounds great." He slung his backpack over one shoulder and leaned down to kiss me on the cheek.

Sharing a late morning breakfast had become a favorite ritual for both of us, a chance to share thoughts and feelings around the warmth of the kitchen table.

Kelly was changing, growing, becoming his own person. His Christian beliefs and values, continuously challenged at the liberal state college, forced him to grapple with issues and philosophies new to him. I found myself listening with motherly pride as he struggled to maintain his spiritual integrity while attempting to put all the pieces of life's puzzle together.

Seeing him mature, emerging into manhood, I realized our relationship had to change, too. I would need to stretch past my familiar role as parent and begin to relate to him, one adult to another. It would mean trusting him in new ways: accepting our separateness, not being threatened if our opinions or life styles weren't the same.

It would also require nurturing a friendship fulfilling for both of us: going to coffee shops where the hair styles were as varied and exotic as the coffee beans and staying up until three in the morning watching another "sci-fi" movie for what seemed like the hundreth time.

This time would also involve risk.

"Yo, Mom, I'm back." Kelly shut the door with his usual heave-ho. "Boy, everything smells terrific, I'm starving." He snatched some potatoes from the plate and slithered them into his mouth with the deftness of a pickpocket. "What are we going to talk about? Did I do anything wrong?"

"Guilty conscience?" I teased. I wasn't anxious to hurry into my confession. I wanted the mellow milieu of the morning to girdle us. The risk I was about to take could cost me his respect, possibly his love. It meant shattering any illusion he might have had of my being the infallible parent.

"I want to explain what's been happening to me lately." I carried the plates to the table. "But let's eat breakfast first."

Finally, unable to avoid the reason for our meeting any longer, I ventured forth with my confession.

"Kelly, I know you've been concerned with my sadness the past few weeks." I halted. I threw my head back and looked up to the ceiling before I let the words spurt out.

"Eleven years ago, just before Dad and I got our divorce, I had an abortion." The sound of the word was like a bullet ricocheting around the room.

"How could you do that?" Kelly shouted. Shock then anger crossed his face as the truth of my words sank in. Our relationship was based on mutual honesty and trust. I hadn't anticipated the obvious pain he would experience. Had I gone too far?

"I've always wanted a brother or sister," he said, fighting back tears. "I can't believe you took that away from me."

Now the shock was mine. It hadn't occurred to me that my decision would deny my only child a heartfelt desire I never knew he had.

"Why, Mom, why did you do it?" His eyes spoke of

betrayal. He had often defended the right-to-life issue, but suddenly the issue had a face on it that he recognized.

"Nothing I can ever say can justify what I did," I began. "When I found out I was pregnant, Dad and I were going through a tough period in our marriage, and he said he didn't want another child, at least not then."

"How old was I?" He searched for a baseline of understanding, a time frame he could relate to.

"You were seven."

"Were you in the hospital?" His question reflected his first hint of recollection. "I remember coming to see you. Dad and I brought you flowers and candy." He remembered.

I turned my head away from him. I wondered how he felt at that moment. Had his memory of visiting me in the hospital made him feel somehow like an accomplice?

"I'd always wanted another child," I continued, my mind drifting back over the memories so long ago pressed down, hidden. "But the timing never seemed right. When Dad said he didn't want another baby, I was angry with him and afraid of losing him at the same time."

His next question jerked my head back to face him. "Mom, did you want me when I was born?"

I reached over and placed my hand on his cheek. Tears welled up in his eyes. "I don't think we stopped smiling the whole nine months I carried you," I said softly, looking directly into his brown-green eyes so earnest, yet so bruised. "We'd tried for almost a year before I finally got pregnant." I realized my confession was casting a shadow of doubt on every phase of past security. "We love you, Kelly. Both your dad and I love you very much."

"Did he know you were doing it, the abortion I mean?"

"Yes. Once it was over, we never mentioned it again. Eight months later Dad and I separated."

I paused to look at my son, a man coming into his own.

126

His jaw was set. I could see him swallowing hard, forcing the tears down his throat like a bitter medicine.

"Shortly after I became a Christian, I realized what I'd done was wrong. I asked God to forgive me. I failed myself by denying what I really wanted, and I suppose I failed your father by not insisting that we accept our responsibilities as parents."

My eyes drifted away from his, I could no longer bring myself to face him. I wanted to run. "I grieved my sin, but it wasn't until last October that I began to mourn the death of my baby." The words caught in my throat.

I waited for my words to be absorbed. "It's only been in the last few weeks that I've allowed my sorrow to be expressed."

"Is that why you've been crying so much lately?"

"Yes, I've needed to say good-bye to a lot of dreams I once had. Honey, I never thought for a minute I would be hurting you." I was beside myself with the awareness. Tears spilled down my cheeks. "Please forgive me, I'm so sorry."

"I'm really trying to understand, Mom," he said, slipping his chair around to hug me. "I do forgive you." We clung to each other tightly and cried, deep remorseful sobs. Strangely, my son's grief comforted me. Now we shared a common loss. I found tears were a special grace.

What was lost? A big brother's comfort, a little sister's love; the hurts, joys, and warmth of family. Oh sure, the two of us were still a family, but what additional depth would this person have brought to both our lives? We would never know.

That day became a watermark for me, as a mother in relationship to her son, and for me as a woman. No longer content with simply knowing the circumstances surrounding my abortion, I wanted to know the deeper reason: why

had I denied my own womanhood, the very core of who I was?

I made a mental note to get in touch with Kathy, the woman I met at Mt. Hermon.

"Kathy, this is Pat Bigliardi, from the Mount Hermon writer's conference," I explained as I recognized her voice on the phone.

"Gosh, I'm so glad you called. I was just addressing the notices for our support group meeting next week. Do you think you'll be able to come?"

"That's exactly why I called. I've been going through a new phase of grief, Kathy. I need to talk to other women who've gone through an abortion, like yourself."

"We have just what you need, Pat. It looks as if there will be around five or six women next Tuesday. We'll be meeting at six o'clock for a potluck dinner."

Driving up Highway 280 toward Redwood City, I passed familiar landmarks: the white church off Magdelane Avenue, the Stanford linear accelerator tunneling its way across the countryside, cows grazing amid radar towers, microwave dishes, scrub oaks, and willow trees. I looked forward to the evening. Many of the phases I'd gone through I had read about, but I sensed my recovery wasn't complete.

The neighborhood Kathy lived in was shaded by large weeping willows, stately sycamores, and elms on each side of the street. Built in the '40s and '50s, the homes were well-cared for. Kathy opened the screen door as I walked up the steps.

"We're just getting started. Did you have any trouble finding us?" She gave me a warm smile.

Large, overstuffed funiture reflected her unpretentious manner. Handmade throws, a redwood burl table, flowered pillows, baby toys, and teenage paraphenelia were evident from the moment I stepped in.

"Pat, let me introduce you to everyone. This is April, Julie, Priscilla, and Nancy," she said as she moved around the room. "Nancy is finishing her masters in marriage and family counseling and acts as our adviser."

Their immediate smiles and greetings put me at ease. Our eyes met knowingly. If only for a few hours, each of us would be with other women who understood without explanation. I was glad I came.

The women sitting casually around the room looked as if they belonged to any other neighborhood coffee-klatch.

April, still in her 20's, brimmed with energy; a bright smile, fashionable haircut, and stylish clothes shouted a youthful confidence. Priscilla, a statuesque middle-aged blonde, whose vowels dawdled in the familiar rhythm of her southern upbringing, looked proper in her lace collared Laura Ashley dress.

Julie resembled a frightened small child with big, sad, almost black eyes and dark brown hair tucked behind each ear. She sat curled up with her feet folded under her in an overstuffed chair, looking as if she wanted to disappear into its wide protective arms. Nancy, an unassuming woman in her 30's, extended her hand toward me.

"We're so glad you could join us, Pat. Kathy told me about you when she got back from the writer's conference."

Instantly, I felt at ease.

The front door opened hesitantly. "Sorry I'm late." A bouncy-haired, attractive young woman apologized.

"Debbie! We're glad you made it."

Vivacious and gregarious, Debbie charmed everyone with her exuberant air of squeaky-clean innocence.

"Pat, this is Debbie. She drives all the way from San Francisco to be here." Kathy reached up to give her an amicable hug before she turned to the group.

"Okay, everyone, grab yourself something to eat. We're just about to get started."

After dinner, Kathy opened the discussion. "Tonight, since we're all at different stages in the healing process, and we've only been together a few sessions, let's begin our discussion by reviewing our purpose for being here.

"This a safe place for each of us to remember the pain associated with our abortion and to look at some of the issues associated with our experiences—the initial trauma, and any guilt, anger, or grief we've felt since it happened.

"Our main objective is to come to a point where we can experience forgiveness and where we can learn new ways to cope with the ongoing reminders of our abortion.

"Let's open the discussion with this question: Have any of you noticed a change in the way you handle situations, the way you approach a decision since you've had your abortion?"

My curiosity was piqued by the question. I listened intently as the other women began to speak.

"I have a real hard time making any decision. I tend to vacillate for days over the simplest things." Debbie paused to gulp a quick bite of potato salad before continuing. "One day I say I'm going to do something, the next day I've changed my mind." She looked up from her plate, her fork in midair. "I think I've had a hard time making any decision since my abortion."

I sat thinking about what she said. Had my own decision-making ability changed since my abortion?

"Debbie, why don't you tell us a little bit about how you came to decide to have an abortion in the first place."

"Oh, wow." She lifted her eyebrows, put her hand to her chin, and took a deep breath.

"Chris, my boyfriend at the time, and I had been dating for about two years. We started sleeping together because

we planned on getting married once he got his divorce. At least that's what he said before I got pregnant.

"I got careless about taking the pill, so when I told him, he told me he'd pay for an abortion, but he couldn't get a divorce, not yet anyway. He said there was no way he wanted to be a dad, at least not now.

"I got scared. I didn't want to lose him, I mean I really loved the guy. So I went to Kaiser Hospital in San Franciso and had it. Then things went from bad to worse. He decided he wanted to try to make his marriage work. It was the pits. I mean the whole thing just pisses me off. I'm still angry at him."

April glanced at Debbie before she looked down at her two hands, rubbing them together as she brushed away invisible crumbs. "My husband almost lost patience with me over my hesitance at having another child. When I was pregnant with our first child, I didn't enjoy it. I was afraid God was going to take my baby from me.

"I didn't understand why I was so fearful until I held my baby in my arms for the first time. Then I remembered my abortion. I had so repressed my experience that I was in complete denial." An edge crept into her voice, hinting at the anger just below the surface. "I can't decide if I can go through it again."

Later I learned that April was 16 when she became pregnant. Once her mother found out she immediately made arrangements for the abortion. Before April knew what was happening she was in the hospital gulping down valium and being wheeled off to surgery. Although never consulted, she had wanted to keep her baby.

"What gave my mother the right to terminate my pregnancy without even once asking me what I wanted? Why didn't my boyfriend stop me?" The pain was evident in her voice.

Glancing around the room, I noticed Julie sitting with her shoulders bent forward, biting her nails. The somber look in her eyes reflected the war raging inside.

"Neither of my parents know about my abortions," Julie confided. "I've had two. They wouldn't understand—they're Catholic. They raised me to be a 'good' girl. That means not having sex before you're married. They'd be so disappointed in me."

Debbie interjected. "I know what you mean. My Dad's very 'old country.' He'd kill Chris if he knew what happened. And I don't want to think about what he'd do to me if he knew what I did."

Julie continued. "I can't trust myself any more with any kind of decision; I panic whenever I even think about what I did. Even at work, I don't say too much to the other women." She spoke more to herself than anyone else in the room. "I let them have their own way about stuff. Then I'm not responsible for anything."

Julie kept staring at her nails, stopping to gnaw at some minute flaw she found.

Kathy reached over and gently placed her hand on Julie's arm. "Julie, why don't you tell us what happened to you?"

Julie looked up for the first time, her eyes fixed on Kathy. Everyone waited in silence. We all sensed patience would be required before Julie could gather the emotional energy to tell us her story.

"My dad had a business associate, a prominent man from San Francisco who had a son a few years older than me. I was 15 and my parents were worried about my lack of social activity. Compared with my older sister I was really shy.

"They all thought it would be nice for me and this man's son to get to know each other. He was 19, handsome and

popular. My parents arranged an elaborate dinner party and invited his family specifically so we could meet.

"A few days later he called and asked me out. I was really surprised. I couldn't believe someone like him would even consider asking me for a date."

For a brief moment, Julie looked away wistfully. "My mom was so excited, she took me out and bought me a new dress." The memory caused her to smile for the first time all evening. "This guy was really nice at first, but by the end of the date he kept pushing himself on me, insisting I make out with him."

Her eyes grew wide; a certain tone slipped into her voice. "I wanted to please my parents and I wanted him to like me, so I let him touch me. Before that night, I'd only kissed one or two boys a few times."

"How did you feel after you let him touch you?" asked Nancy.

"I don't know." She shrugged her shoulders. "I guess I felt good about it. I mean, I thought he really liked me."

She looked up to see if she still had our approval. "He called me again and we went out a few more times. Each time he pressured me to have sex with him. Finally I gave in. Then he never called me again."

Anger rose up in me as I sensed the deep wound that cut a wide swath of pain in this young woman's life.

"When I found out I was pregnant, I didn't tell anyone. I just called Planned Parenthood and arranged for the abortion. I never told him what happened."

We sat in silence. Julie's fragility left us all lost in our own thoughts.

"I had another abortion when I was 21," she said in an apologetic whisper. Her dark eyes darted around the room again as she watched our reaction. "After that one, I went into such a state of depression I had to be hospitalized. I

was in a mental hospital for almost six months. My parents still don't know about either abortion."

"Don't you think it might help them to understand all that you're going through if they knew the truth?" Kathy asked gently.

Julie's body recoiled into the overstuffed chair. "No, I don't want them ever to know what happened." She shook her head in quick short jerks.

Each woman sat staring at the bird-like young girl. Sadness draped itself loosely over the gathering.

Appalled by the undeniable devastation that shattered this frail child, I searched for answers, for understanding. *Dear God, how in the world has this all happened? What have we done to ourselves?*

As the tragic tapestry of each woman's life unfolded that night, deceit and betrayal were common threads.

Priscilla told us she had had two abortions 30 years before in a small cabin in the backwoods of Georgia.

"Back in my day, if you got pregnant and weren't married, you were the talk of the town." Her eyes scanned the room. "'If you're smart, you just do something about it,' my mother warned me. So when I got pregnant at 16, I didn't tell her. My boyfriend made all the arrangements." She sighed. "I'm not proud of my behavior, I guess you'd say I have a sordid past."

Priscilla, a Christian for six years, struggled to remove the mask of respectability she had hidden behind for so many years. She sat erect, legs crossed, her slender, well manicured hands overlapped on her knee.

"We all have sordid pasts, honey." April quipped.

Priscilla chuckled. "I suppose so." She raised her shoulders and tucked her head between them, her sparkling blue eyes reacting to the obvious humor in April's remark.

Priscilla had another abortion at 18, before moving to

California. She remained single for 46 years and now she was engaged to a man in her church.

"For over 30 years, I kept my secret hidden. I've told Howard, my fiance, my pastor, and all of you, of course." Self-consciously, she gestured around the room.

"Until Kathy came to our church and spoke about her abortion, I hadn't given much thought to my bouts of depression and unexplained crying spells. I'd go through times of feeling hopeless. I had boyfriend after boyfriend. I wanted to love someone and be loved in return, but each time my fear of getting hurt again would undermine the relationship," she continued. "I'm not proud of the life style I lived then." She squeezed her hands into tight fists.

"When I became a Christian six years ago, I began counseling with my pastor. He taught me how much God loved me. I met Howard about two years ago and we've been dating ever since. Then, when Kathy told us about post-abortion syndrome, I began to connect my feelings with my abortion.

Priscilla opened her hands, stretching the fingers apart. "You see, my depressions occurred at the same time every year. Those times coincided with the dates of my abortions."

I was fascinated by Priscilla's insight.

She turned toward the overstuffed chair. "Julie, I want to thank you for sharing your story tonight. I think I'm beginning to understand why I've had such a hard time setting a date for my wedding. I think I've been so hesitant because I've been afraid. For years I've probably sabotaged my relationships. What if my decision to marry Howard would end up being as wrong as all those other bad decisions I've made over the past 30 years?"

"All of us suffer from wrong decisions we make. And we will continue to make them." Kathy swept her hand

across the room. "But we have a way of redeeming our errors. We can simply ask God for forgiveness.

"Of course, as we all know, there are consequences as a result of our actions." She raised her shoulders and spread her hands wide to emphasize her point. "We can't always restore those things that have been destroyed because of wrongful patterns in our lives, but the Bible promises us we can start fresh each morning. We can begin to establish new patterns, healthy patterns, patterns of living that God has laid out for us in the Bible."

Everyone listened attentively to Kathy, yet I could tell Debbie was still hesitant to accept the gift God offered her.

"I don't want to change the way I live." Debbie's determination to be self-sufficent squawked its defiance.

"What do you mean?" April spoke abruptly. "Then why in the world are you here?"

Debbie's eyes grew cold. "I love my boyfriend, Jim. He's different than Chris was. I know we're going to get married someday, but right now we can't afford it."

"Isn't that what you said Chris told you?" April's persistence was making me uncomfortable, but Kathy let it ride.

Debbie didn't answer at first. "He's nothing like Chris I tell you," she said shaking her head. "He's tender and considerate." Her shoulders straightened. "I don't see anything wrong with living with him."

"Then why haven't you told him about your abortion?"

"I'm just not ready to tell him." Debbie's voice took on a defensive edge.

Kathy pressed her further. "Have you told your father you're living with Jim?"

"Are you kidding? No way! I think he suspects we're sleeping together, but he's never come right out and asked. I guess he feels what he doesn't know won't hurt him."

"Why do you think it would bother him to know you're living together?"

"Because I'm still his baby girl. He's probably afraid I'll be hurt somehow."

"Like you have been in the past?"

Debbie shook her head, "This is different."

"Debbie," Kathy asked gently, "why do you think the Bible teaches us not to have sex with someone before marriage?"

Debbie simply shrugged her shoulders.

"Do you think it could be for the same reason your dad doesn't want you to live with Jim, because God, our heavenly Father, doesn't want us to get hurt?"

Debbie pressed her lips together tightly. I could sense she had begun to rebuild a wall of resistance around herself.

"Debbie, God is the One who created us, He knows what we can handle and what we can't." I ventured forth. "If you were to buy a red hot Ferrari, let's say, then proceeded to put sand in the gas tank, would it be able to perform to its fullest potential?"

She looked at me inquisitively.

"Let's assume we're like that Ferrari. And God is the Master Designer. He knows the best way we can meet our potential, because He knows how He's put us together. And He's given us an owner's manual, the Bible, just like Ferrari or any other manufacturer provides. If we don't follow the owner's manual, then we can't complain if something goes wrong with the product."

Debbie listened, but I wasn't sure she heard what I said.

"Oops, our time is running out," Kathy said diverting the attention away from Debbie. "Does anyone want to share something she's learned tonight about herself and her abortion experience?"

The evening drew to a close, and the clatter of dishes and hum of voices filled the room. We embraced, kissed cheeks, and patted each other. Kathy hugged me and whispered, "How'd you do tonight?"

"I'm glad I came." Jamming my hands into my pockets, I shook my head in disbelief. "It was a little overwhelming to hear everyone's story."

"I'll call you." She stroked my arm like a mother. In the solitude of the night's blackness during the long drive home, I reflected on the events of the evening. Questions kept popping to the forefront of my mind. I knew the statistics: over 25 million women in America alone had experienced an abortion. Now, for me, those numbers had faces. How many other women were like us, struggling with the consequences?

I tried to sort out the range of emotions I was feeling.

I was confused by the diversity of our experiences when there also appeared to be so many common threads. I was angry because I could see and hear the devastation in each of us, and I wanted the pain to stop for me and for the women I met. And I was frustrated because I was aware that repetitive patterns of self-destruction were still affecting many of us.

Would we ever feel whole? Would we be able to live healthy lives again? The most persistent question that hounded my thoughts still had no answer: Why, why had we allowed these things to happen to us in the first place?

INSIGHT QUESTIONS FOR CHAPTER 8

1. Describe your spiritual understanding at the time of your abortion.

2. Did you have any inner misgivings about your abortion that you experienced beforehand? Read Ephesians 4:17-19.

3. Colossians 1:21 says we were once alienated from God and our behavior and choices reflected our separation from Him. Would your life style at the time of your abortion reflect such an alienation? Describe your life style at the time of your abortion.

4. If you haven't already done so, find a faithful friend or family member and share your abortion experience. Ask her to pray with and for you.

9
...

Breaking the
Chains that Bind

*Free yourself from the chains on your neck, O
captive daughter of Zion!* (Isa. 52:2 NIV).

Spring's extravagance of color yielded to the muted
tones of a hot, dry summer earlier than usual. The foothills
wore broad swatches of golden brown dabbed with drab
green scrub oak. The azure cloudless sky turned murky
with streaks of red-orange and brown smog. The long
California drought continued.

It was the middle of July. The scorching heat prompted
Kathy to suggest a barbecue for our monthly support
group meeting. Outside, the patio air was smudged with
the pungent smoke of burning charcoal. A grill glowed red
hot, and sizzling meat hissed in the night air.

Beyond the Hidden Pain of Abortion

New members had joined the group. Claudia, a bashful woman, had only recently remembered her abortion. So traumatized by her experience, she had repressed it for 15 years. Forced to take a leave of absence from her job due to recurring health problems, she began to have unexplainable flashbacks: sexual advances she struggled to physically thwart, a sense of sadness associated with hospital scenes for which she had no reference point, an overall feeling of melancholia.

Over months she was able to piece together a teenage romance that led to a crisis pregnancy and an abortion. She was referred to Kathy and our support group by her psychologist.

Kim was a young friend of mine. Strikingly attractive, her exotic facial features were highlighted by almond shaped brown eyes. Always a quiet, introspective child, she had become involved in a life style of promiscuity and substance abuse, a radical change in the past two years.

One evening, in early June, I shared my abortion experience at a Bible study in her sister's home. Her sensitive reaction to my story gave me the courage to approach her.

"Kim," I asked discreetly, "have you had an abortion?" At age 20 she had had not one, but two. I invited her to join our support group.

Emily was a perky, outgoing woman with delicate Filipino features who had been in Kathy's support group in the past. Her ability to laugh readily added a light-hearted dynamic to the group.

Faced with another failed relationship and the sole care of a four-year-old daughter and an infant son, Emily recognized that her continued self-destructive behavior revealed her need for further healing.

Some of us were seated around the picnic table, complete with red and white checkered tablecloth and yellow

bug repellent candles, munching on tortilla chips. Others lay casually on chaise lounges, their feet propped up and their eyes closed.

"We've been getting together for a few months now and some of you have said you're having a hard time forgiving those who were involved in your abortion as well as yourself," Kathy said. "Why don't we start with the concept of forgiveness. What does it mean to you?"

"I guess it's letting go of anger and hurt." Debbie stood up to grab a handful of chips before sinking back on her chaise lounge. "But, you know when we talk about forgiveness I feel like I'm having to give one more thing to Chris and I've given him so much already."

"Yeah, I know what you mean. When I think about the way my boyfriend insisted I get an abortion or he'd leave, then he walked out on me anyway, I still get furious. Why should I forgive him? You know what I mean?" Emily's voice was fragile as a bud vase.

"But how does forgiving him seem like you're giving him something?" Kathy probed a little deeper.

"It's as if when I say, 'I forgive you,' I'm saying what he did was okay, and yet what he did hurt me."

April began, "It's taken me a long time to give up my anger. Forgiving my mom meant I had to let it go, and I wasn't sure I wanted to, but about six months ago I finally told her how much I was hurt by what she did.

"We'd never talked about my abortion once it was over. It was like it never happened. In someways not talking about it added to my pain."

"What did she say when you told her how you felt?"

"She said she was sorry it hurt me, but she did what she thought was right at the time. 'You were only 16,' she said, like that was supposed to make it all right. She just doesn't get it. My baby is gone, but she says what else

should she have done?" April's disappointment draped itself across her shoulders.

"But I decided if I was going to get healthy, I'd have to let my anger go. I needed to forgive her, to accept her reasoning, even if I would have handled it differently."

"I think I forgave my ex-husband when I realized I never told him how much I wanted the baby. Sometimes I can't help wondering what would have happened if I'd been honest." My words were wistful patches in my 'if only' quilt.

"I know what you mean. I hated Chris for a long, long time for not wanting our baby. Even now, when I'm alone or I start to think about how he treated me, I get mad all over again," Debbie continued slowly, then paused. "But lately I've been wondering if he's the one I'm really angry with."

"That's good, Debbie." Nancy had been sitting quietly, listening intently before she heard Debbie's response. Pulling herself upright, she joined in. "Because until we can identify who our anger is directed toward, we can't release it, and the freedom forgiveness brings can't occur."

Nancy closed her eyes as if to see more clearly, "Forgiveness is our letting go of the chains we've wrapped around our emotions in a form of self-protection." She stretched her arms wide to emphasize her words. "It's ourselves we're really setting free when we forgive someone."

We all paused. It was as if we needed time to visualize the meaning behind her words.

"I remember being so furious during the months between my abortion and our separation. Yet, until I started coming out of denial, I never linked my abortion to my inner rage." I stopped, suddenly remembering my contorted face in the bathroom mirror the night Kelly stormed out of the house.

"One day I wrote in my recovery journal, 'I'm so angry. . . .' Then I had to stop. I was too afraid to look my anger in the face. It took me months to finish that sentence."

"Boy, do I understand that." Debbie's head shook up and down vehemently. "Sometimes, when I think about what happened, I almost shake with rage."

"What do you do then?"

Debbie looked surprised at Nancy's question. She threw her head back and ran her hand through her thick auburn hair. "I usually go out and get stoned."

"But we can't escape from ourselves, can we?" Nancy asked gently. "Sooner or later we have to come down."

Nancy looked toward the women seated at the table. "How do the rest of you deal with your anger?"

"I withdraw," said Claudia. "I think that's why I've had so many health problems. I just stuff all my anger down inside."

"I just get even." April's quick remark spun the group's laughter into the center of the patio.

When the laughter died down I said, "You know, listening to Claudia I realized something. Just because I yelled and screamed didn't mean I wasn't still stuffing my anger."

"You're right, Pat, it didn't." Nancy smiled at my new-found insight.

"Okay, how do we deal with our anger toward ourselves?" Kathy glanced around the room. "For example, how do you get even with yourself, April?"

"I was just joking, but that's a good question. I mean, in a way we get even when we punish ourselves, right?"

"Okay, let's list some of the ways we might punish ourselves?"

"Not taking care of our bodies." Claudia jumped on the question like a child who finally had the right answer. "Not resting when we need to, not eating right."

"Getting involved with men we know are not good for us." Emily's accent stretched the word *good* out like a piece of saltwater taffy.

Our laughter bounced back and forth. "Drinking too much," Kim answered with her eyes still closed.

April jumped up and stroked the air with her hand like the ringmaster at the circus. "Hey, everyone, Kim *is* awake. I thought we'd lost you, kid." Laughter stirred the air again.

"Don't worry, I never miss a word." Kim's hands gripped the arms on the chaise lounge as she pulled herself up to a sitting position.

"Not allowing anyone to love me?"

The barely audible question pushed itself out of Julie's mouth.

We stopped talking and turned our heads toward her. Perched on the edge of one of the picnic benches, she was leaning against the table with her forearms folded in front of her.

"Tell us what you mean." It was as if Kathy placed her hands in front of the rest of us like a traffic cop so we would give Julie time to continue.

Julie lifted her hand to her chin and looked up, away from us for a minute. "I know God's forgiven me, but I still feel guilty." Her soft voice rose slightly. "I don't think I've forgiven myself, so I'm not sure I let anyone get too close to me." She looked around hesitantly. "Does that make sense?"

"Yes, it does," Kathy answered for us. "Have you thought about why you're afraid of getting too close to anyone?"

"Maybe I'm afraid I'll hurt them, like I did my babies."

Julie's remarks loitered in the crevices of my mind. Intellectually I understood and accepted God's forgiveness, but hidden in my subconscious, in the center of my soul,

was a nagging, unrelenting sense of guilt. Hadn't I really committed an unpardonable sin? How could God still love me? It was then that I knew the one person I hadn't forgiven was myself.

When I returned home, I lay awake, staring into the night's shadows. The bitter gall of guilt thrust its way up into my throat; I felt like vomiting. My daughter was in heaven with Jesus. Someday I would meet her face-to-face. I dreaded the possibility.

What would I say to her? Sorry, daughter, I was too fearful of rejection to express my real anger and hurt, so I aborted you. How could she ever forgive me?

Dear Jesus, please tell my baby I'm sorry. Tell her how much I really loved her, how much I miss her.

A few days later, my car radio was tuned to a Christian station where the *Focus on the Family* broadcast was aired. Hosted by Dr. James Dobson, the program that day was a fictional story about an aborted child's encounter with its mother. I listened almost absent-mindedly at first. Then I could hear my own deep seated fear and guilt mirrored by the mother in the story.

Through the car speakers, a child's voice spoke clearly, "I forgive you, Mommy. I don't hurt any more. I'm waiting to see you. I love you, Mommy."

Although I knew it was a part of the program being aired, I recognized the compassion of my heavenly Father. He arranged for me to hear the words of forgiveness in the small, humble voice of a child. How precious, how tender was my God to have been mindful of such a small detail as this!

I pulled to the side of the road, stopped the car, and rested my head on the steering wheel. It was several minutes before I knew what I had to do next. My self-punishment needed to come to an end. I accepted my own

culpability for my abortion and now I needed to release my anger toward myself and accept not only God's forgiveness, but my own.

I heard my voice say, "Pat, I forgive you." Somehow, I knew I needed to etch the sound of those words into my memory. The peaceful presence of Jesus filled the car. I sat still and quiet in His nearness.

Over lunch one day, my friend, Patti, shared a special moment in her life with me.

"Twenty-five years ago, I gave up my infant daughter for adoption." She rushed on to explain. "I had gotten pregnant at 15. Her father and I knew we were too young to care for our baby properly, so we arranged for her to be placed with a couple unable to have children of their own. Later, we got married, had Patrick and Erin, but over the years I longed to see my firstborn."

Her expression reflected the hidden scanning of children's faces she made over the years. "I wondered what she looked like, if she was well cared for and happy, what her favorite colors were, had she married, did she have children, all the thoughts a mother has about her child."

Patti's round blue eyes glistened, and she pulled a wisp of blonde hair to the side of her face. "About two years ago I decided I'd try to locate her. Once I discovered she was living north of here, I arranged to have an intermediary contact her to see if she was interested in meeting me. Of course I was apprehensive—I had no idea what her feelings might be.

"Just last week we met for the first time." Patti's smile was a broad crescent of white on her face. "We had already exchanged pictures through the mail and decided to meet in a hotel lobby located between our two homes. The

moment she saw me she ran over and wrapped her arms around my neck."

The quiet joy of fulfillment rested a moment between Patti and me.

"Do you know what her first words were? 'I've waited all my life to meet you. I've always wanted to tell you I love you.'"

My hand reached across the table and rested on hers. As the morning sunshine poured over her shoulders, it gathered both of us into its embrace. Minutes fled by. I knew God had arranged this luncheon as a loving, thoughtful gift: My first meeting with my daughter, a divine appointment scheduled in eternity, would be surrounded by the same rejoicing as it had been for Patti and Maureen on earth.

"I want to have a baby, but I'm not sure I want to get married." Kim's fantasy spun sand castles into the darkness as we drove home from our monthly meeting at Kathy's.

I let her remark float out the window into the cool night air.

"Stephen said he'd be willing to be the father." Stephen was her on-again, off-again boyfriend.

"That would be nice of him." I glanced over at her, irritated at first, but seeing her young face, my response softened. "Kim, you know having a baby isn't like playing house when you were a kid."

"I know that." She snapped her head at my patronizing attitude.

"Then am I missing something here? Are you saying you and Stephen are getting married?"

"No-o-o-o." She drew the sound out.

"What then?" My annoyance was back.

"Just what I said. I want to have a baby, but I don't think I want to get married."

"Well, you don't just have a baby. Being a parent means thinking more about your child than about your own needs."

"I'd be a good mother. I know I would."

"I'm sure you would, but Kim it wouldn't be fair to your child to not have a father."

Kim leaned against the passenger door, and I could feel her eyes on me. "Stephen could still be its father, but why does he have to be my husband?"

"Kim, you know your desire to have a baby is a typical post-abortion symptom. We discussed this topic at Kathy's last month. Many women want to have another baby to replace the one they've lost." I fought to keep my voice gentle. "But having a baby just to make yourself feel better, without regard to the baby's needs, is self-centered."

Kim jerked her head away from me. She remained silent for the rest of the drive home.

In early September I received an unexpected call from Kim. She wanted me to meet with her and Stephen over coffee at a nearby restaurant.

She was seated across from Stephen in a quiet booth near the back when I arrived. I slid into the seat beside her and we ordered pie and coffee.

"Pat, I think I'm pregnant."

"Are you sure? Have you had a pregnancy test?"

"No, not yet, but I've missed my period. I think Stephen is the father, but I'm not sure."

"What are you going to do?"

"I'm not having another abortion, that's for sure."

"Good."

I looked at Stephen. "How do you feel about all of this?"

Sheepishly, he looked back at me from under his brows,

his head tucked under. "I hope she's pregnant. I want this baby." A wide grin crossed his face.

Playing with the place mat, Kim wrote the word, *baby*, and children's names she'd chosen on it.

"I want to marry her. I want to be the baby's father even if it isn't mine."

Kim's pen hand paused. "I told Stephen I don't want to get married. I just want to have a baby. He can be its father. I would let him see it all the time, but I'm not ready for marriage."

I decided a little shock therapy might help.

"Stephen, how do you feel about being Kim's stud?"

Grinning-white teeth gave me my answer.

"What if she's not pregnant? What will you two do then? Kim, you and Stephen need to think about your future."

"I want a baby."

"Are you going to continue having sex until you get pregnant? Just saying, 'I want a baby' is not going to cut it. Your relationship needs to be based on healthy decisions, not on trying to compensate for past failures.

"Stephen, are you aware that Kim's abortions are what are driving her to have a baby?"

He shifted before he spoke. "Yeah, I guess so. But I'll be a good dad. I want to be just like my dad. He's always there for us kids."

"Let's assume it's your baby. What will you do if she decides to marry another man?"

"I'm not going to marry anyone," Kim interjected. "I don't ever want to get married." Her voice was adamant.

"Stephen." I looked at him steadily. "She needs you to help her think this through, especially if she is pregnant. You said you want to be like your dad. Well, your dad and mom are godly parents, and so are yours, Kim.

"And where is God in all of this? It comes down to how

you are going to handle your lives, God's way or your own."

They both stared blankly at me. Why should they believe me? Everything around them—movies, television, billboards, music—denied the consequences of pre-marital sex. My voice was muffled by the clamor of sexual freedom's hard sell.

A few days later Kim called to tell me she wasn't pregnant. I could hear her disappointment rub against my relief.

"Kim, this is God's blessing; you and Stephen need help. Why don't you both continue counseling, but go together and be honest with your counselor about your obsession to have another baby."

When I hung up the phone, I knew my words had been impotent. Kim was determined to have a baby and my anxiety for her pushed my mother-buttons into overdrive. My heart ached for both of them. Finally, I acknowledged I could only pray for her and Stephen. In the end, I had to trust God for their care.

The large oversized kitchen at Kathy's was a portrait of an active, caring family.

Red geraniums blossomed outside her kitchen window along with basil, tarragon and rosemary set in clay pots. Proverbs meticulously stitched in needlepoint hung on the walls along with crayola-colored pictures of blue clouds and bright flowers.

Reminder notes strewn all over the refrigerator were held in place by a collection of magnets.

A special play area had been laid out in the kitchen for her foster daughter. Almost three years old, she hadn't started to walk yet. Tom applied his expertise as a carpenter to build props to help develop the little girl's large motor skills. Ramps, small platforms, and stairs, similar to those

used by dancers, were paced in strategic areas. Periodically her cries, screams, and grunts pierced the air.

I watched with awe as this diminutive woman calmly
interpreted the child's attempts at communication.

Kathy poured me a cup of freshly brewed tea.

"Pat, my ministry has been changing. I've been involved in recovery for over 10 years and I suppose I
always will be involved in one form or another. But Tom
and I are in the process of adopting our foster children."

Kathy's loving support had been felt by literally thousands of women through her speaking and writing career,
but she was most fulfilled when she and Tom were caring
for their three birth children and the more than 75 foster
children who had weaved in and out of their lives.

"The special needs of the newborns we minister to have
increased; so many of them have severe physical problems. My responsibilities to them, the Foster Parent Association and the support group are all I can handle.

I put my mug down. "Kathy, I'm amazed you do the
things you do considering the demands the children make
on you."

"Good, because I'm going to ask you a favor. I get all
kinds of speaking requests from groups throughout the
Bay Area. You and April have come the furthest in your
healing process, enough so that I would like to be able to
refer both of you to those who request a speaker."

"Do you think I'm ready, Kathy?"

"I'm sure you are ready. Besides, I've found the more
I've shared my experience the healthier I've become."

It wasn't long before I had an opportunity to test Kathy's
theory.

One morning in early October the phone rang. "Mrs.
Bigliardi? This is Jane Sherlock and I'm the president of
the Ohlone College Christian Club. We're having a forum

on the abortion issue next month and wondered if you'd be willing to speak for us? We've invited the whole campus. It's the biggest event we've ever planned, so we wanted a woman who's had an abortion to explain why she opposes its legalization."

When I arrived, the lecture hall was half full. Young men in jeans, sweatshirts, and baseball caps with their brims turned backwards slouched in their seats. A few middle-aged women in pant suits were a contrast to the young girls in oversized shirts and baggy pants. Soon they would all have one thing in common; their eyes would be focused on me as I stood to speak.

"On Valentine's Day 1976, I had an abortion."

No one moved. I went on to describe how, as a student at San Jose State University, I wholeheartedly embraced such slogans as "Every child should be a wanted child." Yet, eventually I found myself caught in a dilemma of my own rhetoric. I wanted my baby, but its father didn't. I assured them that if abortion had not been legalized, I would never have sought one out.

My voice quivered as I expressed my regret at being given the choice to decide which of my children was to live and which was to die. I said children weren't clones we could cast aside today, assuming we could produce another just like it tomorrow.

I concluded by asking them to consider the long-term consequences of legalized abortion. And I challenged them to remember that as a society we must treasure the life of every child and his or her unique potential if we are to be fully human and fully alive.

As I sat down the audience clapped politely. Ms. Sherlock opened a question and answer session. A young girl dressed in green overalls and military boots stood to speak. "I feel bad for the lady who regrets having an

abortion, but it isn't the same for everyone. If your group really wants to stop abortion, then why don't you support our petition to have condom dispensers in the bathrooms and birth control pills available at the health service clinic?"

Her challenge slapped me across the face. "We believe sex outside marriage is wrong," answered Ms. Sherlock.

"That's the trouble with you Christians," the girl shot back. "You won't tolerate other viewpoints; you're always quoting the Bible. Well, what if we don't believe in the Bible?"

I felt stymied. The young women was right. The real issue was rooted in a person's concept of God and how that belief influenced her way of life.

Through the fall and winter months I continued to speak on college campuses, in churches, at conferences and seminars. The response was always the same: Polite tolerance.

I found myself in a no-man's land.

I was caught between the pro-choice advocates who denied claims of post-abortion trauma and who said any regret was simply a reflection of "religious" guilt and some pro-life advocates who insisted on referring to women who had an abortion as heartless murderers.

Still, each time I spoke, a few brave individuals approached me privately to whisper a confession about their own painful experience. They expressed feelings of betrayal, vulnerability, and woundedness.

In spite of those few, my general lack of effectiveness began to haunt me. There was something about the abortion issue that tapped into a profound aspect of a woman's perception of herself and her place in the world that eluded me.

"Pat, KPIX just called and they are planning on doing a special on post-abortion trauma on their "People Are Talking" show next week." Kathy's voice was excited.

"They wanted to know if I could recommend two women, preferably housewives, to represent the pro-life side of the issue.

"I suggested you and April. There will be two pro-choice women, too."

I was excited about the opportunity, but I also felt the weight of responsibility. I knew only too well that TV talk shows often picked potentially volatile subjects and invited guests from opposing viewpoints to "mix it up" in front of a live and usually vocal studio audience.

Post-abortive women who regretted their decision were usually reticent to discuss their abortion openly. So there was little doubt in our minds that we would find few, if any, vocal supporters in the audience. But we also knew there were hundreds of women in the viewing audience who suffered alone.

"That's exactly why I picked you and April to do it," Kathy spoke decisively. "Remember, our main objective is to reach the silent, hurting women."

"You sound suspicious, are you?"

"I was quite adamant about our desire to remain outside the abortion debate. I told them we were only interested in addressing those women who were having post-abortion reactions and wanted help sorting out their feelings. But I've been stung before, so you and April need to be prepared for the worst. But don't worry. You'll both do just fine. Remember, their objective is to undermine your position. Your main concern is to remain calm when they try to goad you with ridiculous comments or statistics."

My courage was waning quickly.

"I'm trusting God to provide the blanket of peace you'll need to reach out to touch the women who need to know God loves them and can heal them."

We arranged to meet the night before the broadcast at

Kathy's for a strategy session. She would prod us with the type of questions she anticipated would be put to us and we would pray for God's covering and protection.

I called my friend, Diane, and asked if she would drive up to San Francisco with me the day of the broadcast to be my on-site prayer support and to be at least one smiling face in the audience.

We arrived at the studio Monday morning at seven-thirty. One of the producer's assistants greeted us with an aloof smile and engaged us in small talk as the elevator brought us to the fifth floor.

"Please feel free to enjoy the refreshments while you wait," she said, waving at the doughnuts and coffee in the guest lounge.

She then introduced us to the other two participants on the panel. One was a supervisor for the city of San Francisco and the other a professional writer and speaker, both seasoned veterans of talk shows. Then she cautioned us: "We would prefer that the participants not talk to each other before the show. So please don't make any attempt to engage in conversation with anyone other than the staff."

April and I looked at each another in surprise. The ensuing silence became deafening; the air was electrified with the tension that only exists among adversaries. The other two women were pro-choice, each having had an illegal abortion which had caused them a great deal of pain. April and I, on the other hand, had had legal abortions performed in the antiseptic environment of a hospital. Yet, we too had suffered. But today, the commonality of our pain would be ignored and instead there would be an attempt to deny abortion's continued desecration of our womanhood. I was grateful Diane was with me. At least I could talk to her. It would be one-and-a-half hours before

we actually went on the air.

About an hour after our arrival, we began to hear various staff members address the live audience that filed into the studio.

"Do you want them to take away your right-of-choice?" a staff member yelled.

"No," the audience roared back.

"Do you want them to force us back to the days of back street abortions in the hands of butchers?"

"Noooo!" The answer was louder, angrier.

"Should women be made to be baby factories?"

"NOOOOOOO!" The audience was in one massive accord now.

Minutes before the broadcast we were asked to sit in chairs on a revolving platform. Each of us had a microphone attached to our clothes and then we heard, "Ready? Okay, we're live."

The announcer introduced the show, and suddenly the platform began to turn and we were thrust in front of the now cheering audience. Inside I felt like I had just entered the center ring of a Roman coliseum.

The hour show sped by. All four panel members were given time to reiterate their own stories. The supervisor who had an abortion in the 1960's while a college student spoke first. Her illegal abortion had occurred in a dirty, back-street apartment, and an ensuing infection had left her sterile. The writer had her abortion in the late '40s in similar circumstances, which left her emotionally traumatized. Both insisted their abortions had produced sorrow and pain because of the inhumane and careless methods that had been used on them, and they both maintained if their abortions had been legal and performed in the safety of a professional hospital environment, there wouldn't have been any negative consequences. When April and I

were given the opportunity to speak we each reviewed the circumstances surrounding our abortions. Both April's and my abortions were performed legally, yet we each shared how we experienced emotional scars similar to theirs. We both struggled with a deep sense of regret and had experienced feelings of agonizing grief over our loss.

"So are you saying you oppose legalized abortions?" Our host's voice had an incredulous tone to it.

"Yes, I know if abortion had not been legalized I would never have sought one," I answered. "I regret my decision and I have been deeply wounded emotionally by it."

"I know without a doubt I would have kept my baby, but my mother insisted that I have an abortion, and at 16 I didn't feel I had a choice." April's voice was firm and her remarks unequivical.

Members of the audience attacked our pro-life position, but we remained calm in our insistence that for us legalized abortion had brought a sense of never-ending grief into our lives. However, we accepted the fact that all women did not necessarily react to their abortion experience in the same way we had. But we wanted to at least recognize that there were women who did suffer long-range consequences after an abortion, and those women should feel free to acknowledge their regret, without reprisal.

Our ability to focus on the pain and hurt women might experience rather than the political aspect of the issue helped to ease the tension. By being able to relate to all women through the commonality of our womanhood proved to be rewarding. The result was a program which revealed the need for a sensitive and caring approach to the hurt that surrounded the loss of a child, including one lost to an abortion.

After the show the producer, flushed with excitement,

came back stage. "Thanks to all of you, we believe we had a very special show today." The program had taken a path away from the normally explosive nature of the subject and had exposed the potential emotional consequences an abortion could render.

Before we left the studio the writer, who had once seen herself as our adversary, approached April and me.

"I have to admit I've never considered the possibility of grieving the loss of the child." She explained she had gone on to birth two daughers, now both grown, and had only perceived the hurt and regret which surrounded her abortion experience from the viewpoint of the horrifying methods and the painful results her illegal abortion had caused.

"Listening to both of you today I realized I may have repressed my 'mother's grief.'"

April and I nodded knowingly. "We're all women struggling to gain a perspective on the choices we've made in our lives," I said. "That's one thing we share in common."

"I have to admit I hadn't thought of it that way before, she said nodding her head. "Good luck to both of you. I'm glad we've met."

We shook hands and smiled at one another before she turned to leave.

Her remarks encouraged us and we left the studio pleased with the results of our appearance. My own understanding was being broadened by each new encounter, but there would still be much more for me to learn.

INSIGHT QUESTIONS FOR CHAPTER 9

1. Have you had a series of physical or emotional problems since you experienced your abortion? Describe them. How do you think your abortion experience may be related to your current problems?

2. Have you become addicted to drugs or alcohol? Do you think your abortion experience contributed to your substance abuse? Explain.

3. Have you gotten pregnant again to atone for the child you aborted?

4. Have you been trying to work for your forgiveness? Have you become a workaholic or a supermom? List some of the ways you may be trying to atone for your abortion experience.

10

. . .

Silent Wails
of the Heart

He cried out with a loud voice, "Lazarus, come forth!" And he who had died came out bound hand and foot with graveclothes, and his face was wrapped with a cloth. Jesus said to them, "Loose him and let him go" (John 11:43-44).

"I hate him! I hate him!" Kim's words spewed out. "I'll never forgive him. I know what you're going to say, that I won't get better until I forgive him, but I'm telling you I'll never forgive him . . . never!"

She sat stroking her swollen belly. Six months pregnant, she was unmarried, but determined to birth this child.

It was Saturday morning. Ten of us from Kathy's support group sat around the room, ready to share our abortion

story with one another as part of our healing process. Mindful of the time constraints of our monthly meetings, we had set aside this weekend to allow ourselves the luxury of sessions without a clock. We needed to expose the raw roots of our pain in a safe and accepting place.

This was "unfinished business" in our lives. For some, it would be the first time they told anyone all the facts—all the details of the event that scarred their lives. For others, it would be the first time they would be able to remember for themselves what had happened.

Each woman there would be allowed to speak without interruption.

The small cabin in the Santa Cruz mountains provided a warm and homey atmosphere. It had a large living room with a rock fireplace, a prickly mohair couch, over-stuffed chairs with flowered chintz covers, and blue checkered curtains on the windows. When we arrived the evening before, a drizzle greeted us. Now the wind hummed through the giant redwoods, and slanting rain pounded against the windows.

Kim's voice remained detached, a flat monotone, her face devoid of emotion. It was as if she were watching a movie in her mind and was simply describing what she was seeing to the rest of us.

"He just left me there. He drove me downtown to the Women's Community Clinic—you know the one on Santa Clara—and waited for me to get out of the car. It was a little before eight o'clock in the morning."

"Gosh, that's where I had my first abortion." Joan's face showed her shock.

Kim ignored Joan, her eyes fixed on the screen in her mind. "I asked him, 'Aren't you going to come in with me?'"

"Are you kidding? I've got exams today. Anyway, I

wouldn't want anyone to see us here together."

"I watched as his car drove off. I was 17. I'd never even been to the doctor without my mom before. When I opened the door to the clinic, the waiting room was so full there weren't enough chairs for everyone. Girls, some with their boyfriends, were sitting on the floor; others were standing up and down the hallway. No one looked at anyone or said anything, I mean, we all knew why we were there. The nurse took my name and told me they'd call me when they were ready.

"At eight-thirty they started to call groups of women into another room, five or six at a time. I wanted to run, but there was no place to run to.

"I was there an hour or so before my name was called along with five others. A nurse came in and told us to follow her. She led us into a room like a lab or something and asked us to line up. It was like a production line: she pricked our fingers, smeared the blood onto a glass slide, took our temperature and blood pressure.

"While we were waiting, I saw this man dressed in green surgical clothes rush by, blood splattered all over the front. I got so sick I almost fainted. I was so scared."

Her hands cupped her bulging belly, as if to reassure the baby she now carried inside her.

"I wanted it over quickly. I was worried because my parents thought I was in school. I needed to get home before they did.

"After about another hour, I was led into a room. The nurse pulled back the curtain and said, 'Take off your clothes. Tie the gown in the front.' I looked into her eyes. I needed an adult to tell me I was going to be all right.

"'I don't know if I should do this,' I said as I stared into her eyes.

"'Everyone says that. You'll feel better when it's over

165

and you'll go on with your life.' She handed me a pill. 'Here, take this, it will help you relax,' she said. 'After you change you'll need to go in with the other girls. We'll call you when the doctor is ready. He'll be here soon.'

"She was right. The pill she gave me made everything slow down. My body felt heavy. After I was changed, I sat on a couch with two other girls.

"It was probably an hour before they called my name again. I was the last one waiting. They led me into a small examining room, where they told me get up on the table. My feet were placed in stirrups and I waited, alone for a long time. Then the door opened and the doctor came into the room with two nurses. I couldn't see him clearly because I was lying down. He didn't say a word.

"One nurse said, 'This may hurt a little, but don't worry, it will be over before you know it.' She rolled a machine near the foot of the examining table. It sounded like a loud vacuum cleaner.

"Before I knew what was happening, I felt a scraping sensation on the inside of me. I heard a sound as if something was getting caught in the vacuum. A sharp pain surprised me. I began to cry, 'Stop, stop!' But that sound didn't stop.

"I wanted to scream, but I just hung on to the nurse's hand. Finally it was over. I wanted to die. That's when the cramps started. I was so afraid. I thought, I could die right here on this table. The doctor left without saying a word.

Kim closed her eyes and we listened to the rain on the cabin roof. She didn't say anything for a long time. We waited, each of us lost in our own thoughts. Finally, she opened her eyes. They were smoldering with hate.

"I was the last one in the waiting room when Keith finally arrived. I wanted to run to him, to feel his arms around me, pulling me close to his chest like he always

did. He didn't even look at me.

"We walked outside. He opened the car door for me, then said, 'For God's sake you're a mess. You better comb your hair and put on some makeup or your parents will know something happened.' His voice was cold. I bent my head to open my purse. Tears filled my eyes, but I didn't say a word. 'Our baby just died, don't you know that?' I screamed in my head.

"When we pulled up to my driveway, all he said was 'I'll call you.'

"But he didn't call.

"I couldn't tell anyone, not my sisters, my mom, not anyone. I was all alone.

"It was then that I started hating him."

Kim looked up. She had finally left the theater of her mind.

We remained motionless.

Suddenly, Kim started to speak again. "After Keith and I broke up, I really started to party. I'd climb out my bedroom window in the middle of the night to go dancing, then I'd deliberately get stoned. I'd seduce some poor innocent guy, leaning my body against his while we danced, letting my lips brush against his neck or cheek." She threw her head back and smiled in obvious delight. "After I lured him in with my bait, I'd get real cold and tell him what a jerk he was.

"I got a reputation for being a mean, hard cookie, and that's the way I liked it." She lowered her head and stared at each of our faces. Her defiance stood in front of her and dared us to challenge it.

Her grief, masked for so long, waited in a deep crevice of her soul. Unreleased, it would continue to stalk her peace and steal her contentment.

"When I got pregnant again, I was happy and scared at

167

the same time. At 19, I wanted a baby real bad. I didn't want to hurt my parents, but I didn't want to kill my baby. I didn't feel I had a choice.

"I waited a long time, almost three months before I called the clinic for an appointment. When I went in for my first appointment, I decided I couldn't go through with it. They told me to go home and think about it.

" I did, but I knew my parents would be so disappointed in me. The next day I went back. I was still upset, but they said I no longer had a choice. I started yelling. I told them I didn't want the abortion anymore. The doctor got very angry. They gave me a sedative to calm me down, but I kept screaming. I thrashed around trying to get off the table, but the nurses pinned my arms and legs down by leaning on me. Finally they strapped restraints on me. I kept screaming, 'I don't want to kill my baby. Please don't kill my baby.'"

There it was—raw, brutal, naked: a mother's lament. Unheeded.

After dinner we gathered in the living room. Once the hum of our conversation died down, Joan began speaking first.

"When Kim started telling her story I couldn't believe we had had our abortions at the same clinic. I'm probably what—10, 12 years older than you? When I think of all the women who have been through just that one clinic, I get sick.

"You know, until a year ago I had totally blocked out any memory of that abortion. But after listening to Kim this afternoon, I allowed all the pain to resurface.

"I was 22 years old then with two kids, married to an abusive husband. My baby was only 10 months old.

"It was 1976 and the women's liberation thing was real

big: Billy Jean King beat Bobby Riggs in tennis, Gloria Steinem was all over TV talk shows. I knew abortion was legal, and I thought it was socially acceptable, so what could be wrong about it?

"My husband was drinking heavily in those days. He hit me and the kids often. When I found out I was pregnant again I didn't want to bring another child into the mixed-up environment we lived in. One night my husband got drunk and started pushing me around, slapping me across the face. I said, 'If you hit me one more time I'm going to abort this baby.' He leaned back and let me have it right across the face.

"I made up my mind then and there."

Joan looked down and slowly shook her head. "Sounds so stupid when I say it out loud, but that's how I felt about it. I couldn't stand the thought of him hurting this baby like he had the other two.

"My abortion experience was like Kim's. The waiting room was full. The doctor walked in and the only words he spoke during the procedure were, 'I'm finished.' Then I heard him pull his gloves off and walk out.

"Something happened to me that day. My experience changed me on the inside. It changed the way I thought about myself, about everyone else, and it changed the way I thought about life. I was another person. I was able to function, but it was as if I watched me from the outside. For the next 10 years I walked in a gray fog. All the color drained from my life.

"A year later my husband was hit by a car walking across the street and he died.

"I decided to move to Colorado with my two boys. As soon as I got a job, I started having an affair with my boss, a married man, who was 18 years older than me. I was 34.

"I had two more abortions before I swore off men.

Beyond the Hidden Pain of Abortion

"After my last abortion at a clinic, I hemorrhaged badly. It took two girls to hold me down, the pain was so excruciating. I had to have an emergency D & C at the hospital.

"After that, I became the hardest woman on earth. I wouldn't allow myself to be dependent on anyone. I became extremely self-sufficient. I didn't care about anyone but me. I didn't shed a tear for seven years."

Joan's voice cracked for the first time. She bent forward, her arms wrapped around her stomach in preparation for the pain she knew was coming.

"My two older boys really suffered from my problems. They both became substance abusers. My oldest was arrested five times for petty vandalism and was convicted of armed robbery at 14. My youngest was an alcoholic by the age of 12."

Her blue-green eyes clouded over with tears.

"I guess that's the hardest part, seeing how my behavior affected them."

Her words froze in the air. We knew all of our living children also had ultimately been affected by our decisions. Joan's torment was our own.

Many of us held onto our pain, refusing to let it go because our boyfriends, husbands, mothers, fathers, doctors, or pastors had not accepted responsibility for their part in our decisions. But their lives had moved on. Ours remained moored in the muck of unforgiveness. I sensed our need to bring closure to our pain. The lives of those we loved most, our living children, were being distorted by our refusal to forgive.

Then Anne spoke up.

"I don't even know how many men I've slept with and I can't remember how many abortions I've had—I think its six or seven." Anne had remained aloof from the group most of the weekend, choosing to remain quiet and obser-

vant. Until recently, she had been a homeless drifter on the streets of San Francisco. Aged beyond her years, her face reflected poor health.

"I got caught up in the whole '70s drug scene. It started in high school. I lost my virginity at a party when I was 14. I wasn't planning on having sex, it just happened. All my friends talked about how great sex was, but it was no big deal for me. I'm not sure I can even remember the guy's name." Anne looked at April, her mentor, for encouragement.

April smiled and nodded at her to go on.

"The gang I hung around with would party after school and on weekends down in the Haight-Ashbury district of San Francisco.

"When I got pregnant, I just went to the free clinic and had an abortion. My girlfriends did the same thing. We didn't think too much about it. We just thought that was the thing to do. I don't remember it being all that bad." Anne sat back, her voice sad and tired. "But then I don't remember too much of anything any more.

"Two years ago I found myself in a drug abuse clinic. A whole decade of time was gone.

"What really bothers me," her voice trudged on slowly, "is the fact that I can't remember how many abortions I've had. I could have had five or six, maybe seven kids." Anne shook her head in disbelief. "How can somebody's life just slip away? If I didn't believe that God could help me now, I don't think I could face all the pain. I'm 31 years old and I'm beginning to have a real life for the first time."

The harsh facts of Anne's life wrenched our attention toward the self-destruction in her story in a way we couldn't ignore. Although the specifics were different for each of us, we knew the same self-destructive tendencies were present in the lives of every woman there.

Beyond the Hidden Pain of Abortion

Our inability to value ourselves as women made in God's image was becoming more evident.

Kathy broke the silence. "We need to take a break. How are you all doing?"

April jumped up and headed for the kitchen. "Let's pig out. I'm hungry."

The tension was broken as voices filled the air. "Food, a women's answer to everything." "Yeah, let's go see what we can find in the kitchen." "We're right behind you."

Kathy and April brought out a tray of snacks and some soft drinks.

I watched the rain beat against the small squares of glass in the old wood framed windows. A warm fire kept the dampness at bay, but without a phone or a TV it was if we were in a time warp.

I worried about what would happen when we all drove down the mountain the next day, back to our families and all their demands. Would we be able to cope with the raw edges of memory that had been opened this weekend?

Kathy was already prepared for that.

"Before we finish this evening, we'll want to make time to pray for each other. Then tomorrow, let's close our weekend with communion, because the real healing for all of us will come as we allow God to bring His special balm to our wounds. Let's be sure to lay our pain in Jesus's hands."

After we had a time of prayer, we each went to our rooms.

I could hear Kim breathing softly on the bed next to mine, but I tossed and turned, unable to sort out my own feelings of anger and hurt. Slowly I pulled back the covers and threw my feet over the side of the bed.

The springs creaked as I stood up. I stopped for a

second to be sure I hadn't disturbed Kim. She rolled over, but her breathing told me she was still asleep.

The hallway was dark as I gently shut the door behind me. Moonlight cast its glow through the cracks in the livingroom curtains. The rain had stopped.

I tucked my feet under me and sat in the large rocker by the fireplace where a few embers provided just enough heat to keep me warm.

The stories of the women would not leave my thoughts. They seared my mind with the cold reality of their mistreatment. In comparison, my own abortion seemed antiseptic and removed from the experiences of the abortion clinics they described. Still, I searched for a clue in the commonality of our experiences.

Where is the common thread?

Two factors seemed to reappear in every account: the way each woman perceived herself, particularily in relationship to men; and the brutality to which they allowed themselves to be subjected. Where was their self-worth? *Where was mine?* Why had we devalued ourselves? What caused us to negate the very essence of our womanhood? Could the feminists be right? Are we all doomed to devalue our worth until we build an inner tower of self esteem?

My thoughts were too frightening for me to consider, at least for now. Still curled in the rocker, I rocked back and forth, back and forth until I fell asleep.

As I continued to speak at various college campuses, repeatedly I encountered young adults who questioned the validity of abortion's consequences. Discouraged, I began to doubt if my involvement was of any value.

Yet the pain I had seen etched on the women's faces in my support group as each one told me her abortion story was as real as the deepest human experience could be.

173

Was there something I was missing?

My growing concern was finally confirmed one afternoon at Gavilan Community College in Gilroy, California. Once again I was asked to speak at a pro-life information forum. Gilroy, an agricultural community 35 miles south of San Jose, offered visitors pastoral vistas of rolling hills and rich, fertile agricultural soil. The Gavilan campus rested at the base of the foothills on the Southwest side of town.

Joining me on the panel that day was a doctor from a local hospital who showed dramatic in utero slides of a fetus at varying stages of development. During the question and answer period a young woman in the audience approached the microphone and began to address the panel.

"I resent your lies," she began. "You're using scare tactics, telling us those slides you showed earlier are pictures of babies, but that's just fetal tissue."

"My dear young lady, look at the pictures for yourself." The doctor flipped on the projector again. "Certainly you can't deny that is a picture of a baby. Look at its fingers and toes. What would you call it?" The doctor's voice couldn't hide his incredulity.

The young woman stared back at the doctor. "You are wrong," she repeated. "Those photographs are pictures of fetal tissue, not babies. No matter what you say, I know it's just fetal tissue."

I listened, stunned at her insistence that we were trying to deceive her.

On the drive home I was overwhelmed by a truth I had never been willing to accept. Before this encounter, I had always believed in education—that if honest, factual information was presented to normally intelligent persons, it could influence their thinking and ultimately change their behavior.

174

Yet, that day I was an eye witness to a biblical truth: *"The god of this age has blinded the minds of the unbelievers"* (2 Cor. 4:4 NIV). That young woman's mind was closed, she was incapable of seeing truth. And she was representive of the majority of young adult audiences I was addressing on college campuses.

I had to admit that no amount of intellectual prowess or articulate rhetoric would change her perspective. I knew God was the only one who could open her eyes, but I felt frustrated and impotent. I could not seem to communicate the truth of God's character and His plan for us to young people in a way that related to them.

Exposing one of the most intimate and painful experiences of my life to these audiences was preventing few if any abortions. Nor was it convincing young adults to wait until they made the lifetime commitment of marriage before having sex. Why continue? I reasoned.

My own healing from my abortion seemed complete. I had accepted God's forgiveness, had forgiven those involved in my abortion, and had forgiven myself. It was time to put that period of my life behind me. It was time to move on.

INSIGHT QUESTIONS FOR CHAPTER 10

1. Is there anyone in your abortion experience, your unborn baby's father, your parents, friends, you still feel angry with? List them if you can.

Common targets for our anger and bitterness are

    a) Those individuals we believe withheld the truth about the procedure from us

    b) Friends or family members who presented abortion as the best choice

    c) Ourselves for being in the situation where the unplanned pregnancy occurred

    d) The father of our baby for not being there, either physically, emotionally, or financially

    e) Ourselves for not being strong enough to choose life for our babies

    f) God for not stopping us from having the abortion or for not allowing us to get pregnant again

2. Find a quiet place and time to be alone with God. Ask Him to show you areas of bitterness left from your experience(s). Ask Him to prompt your memory with any person you may still be angry with. When that person comes to mind, write an imaginary letter to God. Tell Him you have been angry with that person and the specific ways that person hurt you. This exercise is only a means of bringing light into the darkened corners of our souls, so God can heal any anger or bitterness.

3. Have you examined the ways you may have hurt others at the time of your abortion experience? Ask God to reveal those to you. Write down what comes to your mind.

4. Have you asked God to forgive you for the ways you have hurt others? Stop and pray right now asking God for His forgiveness. Write out your prayer.

11

. . .

So That You
May Know

*I will give you the treasures of darkness, riches
stored in secret places, so that you may know that I
am the Lord, the God of Israel* (Isa. 45:3 NIV).

Three years had passed since my encounter with the
young woman in the college auditorium in Gilroy. The ex-
change between her and the medical doctor about what de-
fined a baby from fetal tissue was a pivotal point in my life.

I didn't want to sit through any more intellectual de-
bates about what constituted a baby. Instead, I wanted to
help others experience the healing I'd received from the
freeing truths of life. I had a burning desire to encourage
others that the God of the Bible was real.

For the first time in my life, building a successful

business seemed insignificant.

After prayer and discussion with my family, I secured a full-time position in ministry, as the director of communications and Christian education at South Valley Community Church in Gilroy.

However, my efforts in ministry still left me unfulfilled and discontented. Somewhere along the line I had lost my relationship with Jesus. The bright primary colors of joy and excitement I experienced as a new believer faded into grayed tones of religiosity.

Finally, while teaching an adult Sunday school class, I found myself admitting my relationship with Jesus was perfunctory. Then I heard myself say, "If my own relationship with Jesus isn't dynamic and vital, then how can I remain in ministry?"

In desperation, after two-and-a-half years in Gilroy I resigned my position.

Then one afternoon in mid-July, I knelt down at the side of my bed and cried out like King David, "Dear God, You said if I didn't know what I was doing, to pray to You, my heavenly Father, because You love helping me. Please restore the joy of my salvation, and show me how I can follow You more completely."

Shortly after my prayer, my sister, Mary, called. She, her husband Craig, and their five children lived in the small community of Truckee, California, high in the Sierra mountains.

"Pat, Craig and I have been praying for you and we think you should reconsider completing your book on abortion recovery."

My voice squeaked in surprise. "Mary, I haven't been involved in abortion recovery for almost three years."

Undaunted, Mary continued. "Thousands of women need to experience the healing you've received, but they feel

too guilty to approach God. You've wanted to impact lives. What better way than to lead women to wholeness in Him? Craig and I want you to consider moving in with us so you'll be free to finish your book without financial pressure."

"Surely, you're kidding!" I was struck dumb by the thought of writing in their cosy home accompanied by five lively children under age 10.

"At least promise you'll pray about it," Mary said.

I hung up the phone muttering, "No way, Jose." Would God really want me to move away from my son and my friends to write a book on a subject I had spent the last three years avoiding?

Over the next few days I prayed for confirmation, but like a modern day Jonah I resisted God's call. I sought my pastor and his wife's advice, hoping they would discourage me from accepting Mary's offer. However, they, too, believed it to be God's provision. Kelly and my sister Lorraine, concurred.

Grudgingly, with my heels dug in and my spirit rebellious, I moved to Truckee. The last place I wanted to be was crowded into a house in the mountains for months on end, dependent on relatives.

My sister's two-story brown saltbox-style home sat on two-thirds of an acre of woodlands. Its 1,800 square foot interior seemed to be filled with active, bosterous children everyday. I tried to adjust to the cold, new church, new friends, and to being completely dependent on my family.

I volunteered to handle the kitchen detail before I realized what it would be like to shop, cook, and clean up for at least eight people every day. I had also not considered the endless mounds of laundry that had to be washed, folded, and put away daily.

The hour-and-a-half of bedtime ritual that five children

required came as another shock: changing into pajamas, jumping on beds, brushing teeth, jumping on beds, saying prayers, jumping on beds, singing songs. . . .

Mary and Craig gave up their downstairs office for me. As the author-in-residence I was the only person to have my own room. Still, I harbored anger at being asked to yield to God's plan for my life.

The rock-hard futon mattress, I was convinced, was a form of penance for the sins of a lifetime. It became the focal point of my disdain.

It wasn't long before living with my sister's family revealed a self-centeredness I hadn't been willing to face. I couldn't help but notice my need to have things my way. Set against the backdrop of five trusting children, my own selfishness cast a black shadow.

Then, early one morning the shadow hovered over me. After carefully preparing breakfast, the anger I felt seeped out toward my nieces and nephew. "Heather, Rachael, Kevin, and Sara, I want you to come to the table immediately. Do you hear me?" No response. I raised my voice.

"I said now!"

Heather, Sara and Kevin wandered to the table without Rachael. In desperation I raised my voice higher. "Rachael, I said NOW." Another minute passed before my eight-year-old niece meandered in. My patience completely spent, I yelled, "While you're taking your good old time coming to the table our food has grown cold. And I hate cold food!"

Tears welled up in her big brown eyes. I could almost hear her saying, "And you call yourself a Christian?" Guilt grabbed my stomach and yanked hard.

Later that afternoon I knelt down beside Rachael so I could look at her face-to-face.

"Auntie Pat needs to ask your forgiveness for yelling at

you this morning." Rachael tucked her chin into her chest and lowered her eyes. "Will you forgive me?"

Tears filled her eyes once again, as she nodded her head yes. But I could see that the damage I had done to our relationship would take time to fully heal.

After that day, I held in my anger for the sake of the children, but its constant menace pressed against my thoughts.

I didn't want to be in Truckee. I didn't want to be bothered by the demands of a young family, and I certainly didn't want to submit myself to the discipline of researching and writing about a subject that now seemed distant and irrelevant to me.

My personal devotional time consisted of crying out to God to release me from this impossible situation. I missed my friends; my son, Kelly; my sister, Lorraine; my home church; and my pastors, Mike and Joyce Woodman. I whined to God about the futon bed.

What kept me from trusting God with my life no matter what the circumstances? If an intimate relationship with God was a real possibility, why did it seem beyond my reach?

Restless and unable to sleep one night I noticed the slim volume, *Experiencing the Depths of Jesus Christ*, on the bookshelf near my bed. I opened it to its simple, inspiring preface:

This little book, conceived in great simplicity, was not written to be published. I wrote it for a few individuals who desired to love God with all their hearts.[1]

I found Madame Jeanne Guyon's opening lines as fresh today as they were in the seventeenth century when she wrote them.

I give you an invitation: If you are thirsty, come to the living waters. Do not waste your precious time digging wells that have no water in them. (John 7:37; Jer. 2:13)

If you are starving and can find nothing to satisfy your hunger, then come. Come, and you will be filled.

You who are poor, come.

You who are afflicted, come.

You who are weighted down with your load of wretchedness and your load of pain, come. You will be comforted.[2]

Throughout her book I saw an undeniable expression of love for Jesus, a longing to know Him, to express her love toward Him.

When I speak of this "deep, inward relationship with Jesus Christ," what do I mean? Actually, it is very simple. It is only the turning and yielding of your heart to the Lord. It is the expression of love within your heart for Him.[3]

Madame Guyon encouraged her reader:

As you come to the Lord pray, bring a full heart of pure love, a love that is not seeking anything for itself. Bring a heart that is seeking nothing from the Lord, but desires only to please Him and to do His will.[4]

Her love for Jesus challenged me. I had to admit I didn't want to yield myself to please God and relinquish my ambition to do His will my way.

Slowly, as I continued to meditate on Madame Guyon's writings, I began to see that Jesus wanted something more from me, much more than mere service. I knew God loved me. But deep within, I began to sense more in my hesitancy to love Him than the act of relinquishing my will.

He desired to have a meaningful relationship with me. Although I had cried out through the years for an intimate relationship with Him, it struck me that I was the one who withheld myself from Him.

Somehow my hesitancy was rooted in a lack of trust in Him. But where did it come from?

Then one day, I remembered an incident with my niece, Heather. She had misplaced my car keys when she was two years old. Looking in every conceivable nook and cranny throughout my apartment, I was at a loss.

In desperation, I knelt down to see the room from Heather's viewpoint. That was when I noticed that the door handle to the linen closet loomed larger and more enticing from my knees. Could the keys be in there? Lying on the second shelf, exactly at Heather's eye level, were the missing keys.

As long as I approached the lost keys from an adult's logical perspective, I was unable to locate them. The prospect of finding keys in a linen closet seemed ridiculous. But Heather was not bound by the same adult logic.

Could my unexplained mistrust of the Lord be like the keys hidden in the linen closet of my child's mind—away from rational adult logic?

I began to journalize my earliest memories in hopes of discovering clues to my distrust. Gradually, bits of memory reappeared.

My father was drafted and sent overseas when I was three months old and didn't return until I was two-and-a-half. His return prompted a difficult period of readjust-

ment for my parents and me.

The pressures of reassimilating into society, finding a job, reestablishing a young marriage, and living with his parents produced a great deal of tension. Numerous arguments raged between my parents. I recalled a number of incidents where I had observed physical violence.

One incident in particular held a place of fixation within my memory over the years, though I had unsuccessfully tried to probe its importance with various counselors.

One day, I watched a small boy looking for his missing father in a bookstore. As he searched up and down the aisles, his little face was stoic, his lips pressed against his teeth. As he turned a corner and saw his father, his face lit up. "Daddy! Daddy!" He began to cry with relief as he ran down the aisle with his little arms flung out, and he was scooped up and held close in his father's arms.

Later, as I recalled the face of the small boy, I remembered the particular scene that had haunted me from childhood.

My parents were pushing and shoving each other around while I sat cowering in the corner of our living room couch. For the first time, in my mind's eye, I saw Jesus standing in the room. I watched as He approached my parents, who were so engrossed in their argument they didn't notice Him.

He turned from them and walked toward me. I felt His strong arms reach down and lift me close to Him. As I recalled that moment I began to sob great tears of relief. Finally I felt safe in His arms. I continued to weep as the fear I had held onto for over 40 years began to drain away.

Significant changes took place within my body after that experience. An inner tension ebbed away, replaced by a new calm and inner peace. My need to control situations began to disappear, and I began to enjoy my family in a

new, relaxed way. As Jesus personified safety in God that night, my child within felt safe in the embrace of her heavenly Father.

Encouraged, I continued to spend long hours reading, praying, and journalizing my findings. I also made time to review my relationship with Jesus over the years.

One particularly cold morning, as soon as I heard Craig building a fire in the stove, I popped out of my room, my morning hair stretched out in all directions with a wild-eyed look on my face. "I've been redeemed!" I shouted.

Mary turned from the coffee pot and looked puzzled. "Pat, you've been a Christian for 16 years. What are you trying to say?"

"I know it sounds ridiculous to you, but I finally understand the full concept of redemption." I paused to reach for the steaming cup Mary offered. "All of my adult life I've been trying to get it together, trying to become a whole person. Last night I realized that no matter how hard I try, I will never fully comprehend life—never have all the answers. Then it hit me. God never intended for me to be whole without Him.

"Last night I realized part of my anger with God has been rooted in my misunderstanding of what I thought God expected of me."

Mary's eyes still had questions. "I'm sorry, Pat, but you've lost me. Why were you angry with God?"

"Because I've been trying to be perfect, to live up to what I thought He expected, to have the answers, to make the correct choices on my own. I was angry because deep down I knew I didn't have all the answers."

Both Mary and Craig started to laugh.

I tried to pat down my shooting strands of hair and continued, "Once I realized those were my expectations, not His, I knew my anger had been without cause. Then I

truly understood that the very nature of redemption is that Jesus Christ paid the price for my mistakes. To expect perfection of myself is putting me on the same level as God."

Mary and Craig cheered and applauded their approval.

After that morning, I sensed another change in my relationship with God. No longer bound by my unrealistic expectations of perfection, I could readily run to Him with my doubts, fears, and hurts.

A new intimacy began to develop between us. Knowing I was accepted by Him just as I was, I came without my anger and frustrations. I began to trust the nature of His character. That was when the first shoots of self-acceptance started to push through the winter soil of my soul.

Shortly after what Mary and Craig called my "redemption revelation," several of Mary's friends in Truckee approached me about starting a post-abortion support group for the women in the area. It had been four years since I was involved, and I decided it would be a good way to immerse myself in the consequences of abortion once again.

Christians in Truckee had established Lifeline, a crisis pregnancy center spearheaded by Merry Hejny and other dedicated volunteers. Because its year-round population of 3,100 swelled during the summer with good-time seekers clamoring to the nearby waters of Lake Tahoe and, during the winter, to the ski resorts, the Truckee area had no shortage of unwanted pregnancies,. Lifeline had an active community outreach.

A few days after meeting Merry, I received a phone call from her.

"Pat, there's a speaker appearing in Reno tonight you might want to hear. Her name is Carol Everett. She was an

abortionist in Texas, and she's written a book about her experiences. I think you should meet her."

The meeting room at John Ascuaga's Nugget casino that night was filled with more than 200 people. Promptly at 7:30 p.m., a diminutive, attractive woman, dressed in a conservative business dress, approached the podium to polite applause. Looking more like a PTA president than an abortionist, Carol Everett began by telling us that, before she ended her career as the director of four abortion clinics in Texas, she had overseen 35,000 abortions in 10 years.

"Abortion is big business," she stated.

The numbers were accurate, she said, because they were directly tied to her personal income: Carol made $25 per abortion; the doctor made $750. She quoted abortion prices that ranged from $250 on up, depending on how advanced a pregnancy was, and other factors.

Quickly, I tallied those figures on the edge of my notepad. Even at $275 per abortion, her four clinics alone would have grossed almost $10 million in that decade.

Carol had been a young divorcee with three children to raise when she began working at the clinics. Driven by her need to justify an abortion she had experienced and the high income potential her position offered, she pursued success with an evangelistic fervency.

Now a Christian, she traveled the country telling audiences about her experience in the abortion industry.

As director of the clinics, Carol had volunteered to speak to young girls at middle schools and junior high campuses as part of the local school district's sex education program.

"I approached schools with one thought in mind: to establish a long-term relationship with potential clients," she said matter-of-factly. "My rapport with young girls

provided me easy access. I knew if they learned to trust us, they would depend on us to provide a confidential and supportive means of securing birth control pills without having to have their parents' consent."

Carol's hands moved quietly to grip the sides of the podium before she divulged the next part of her plan.

"Because I knew teenagers would be lackadaisical about taking the pill on a regular basis, I would have our doctors prescribe a low dose pill which required daily use to be effective. Inevitably, they would become pregnant and come to our clinics for their abortions."

The audience shifted uncomfortably as she continued.

"The average teenage girl becomes sexually active around age 13 or 14, so we reasoned she would probably have at least three unwanted pregnancies before she was 18. We knew we would have a constant source of income."

I sat in stunned silence.

For the first time I was confronted with the possibility that adults, many of whom were medical professionals, knowingly set up young girls to get pregnant, deliberately preying on a young woman's inexperience and vulnerablity for their own monetary gain.

As I listened to Carol, the face of Heidi, a sad-eyed 21-year old in Carson City, Nevada, flashed across my mind. Seated across from me at a conference, Heidi shared that she had experienced six abortions, one a year since she'd turned 16.

I wondered if she had been victimized by a self-seeking opportunist such as Carol Everett had been. Unfortunately, Heidi, and others like her, had little understanding of the reason for the heartbreak they subjected themselves to again and again and again.

INSIGHT QUESTIONS FOR CHAPTER 11

We have learned a great deal about the consequences of our abortion decision: denial, anger, bitterness, depression, guilt, shame, self-deprecation. Now it is time to delve into the events of our lives that led to our self-destructive behavior.

1. What have you done so far in your healing process that you are really proud of?

2. What was your relationship with your mother? Did you feel nurtured and affirmed by her?

3. What was your relationship with your father? Did you feel nurtured and affirmed by him?

4. Was your gender affirmed by your mother? Your father?

5. Early childhood events teach us how to relate to the world. Specific memories from our childhood often reveal the root of our destructive adult behavior. Write one pleasurable and one painful memory that you associate with each person in your family of origin. Be specific and make sure you include any events or abuses that occurred, verbal or physical.

12
...

A Legacy of Life

. . . that you . . . may have power, together with all the saints, to grasp how wide and long and high and deep is the love of Christ (Eph. 3:18, 19 NIV).

Returning from my encounter with Carol Everett, once again I found myself furious with God. I threw myself on the bed and raged against Him for the suffering abortion wrought.

"Let's face it, God. I don't want to have to deal with this abortion issue any more. I don't want to hear one more woman's story, one more confession of the wounds she's been subjected to because of her abortion experience. It's just too painful."

I allowed my deepest hurts to surface and spew out like

bitter gall. "I hate being a woman. Why did You even create me if You knew the wounding and rejection I would have to face because I am a woman?"

After my tirade I lay still on the bed and waited for a lightning bolt to strike me dead. God was sure to zap me now.

What happened next was a surprise. A warm peace settled around me. I could sense God's still, quiet presence. It was as if He whispered to me, "I've always known how you felt, Pat. I'm glad you know it now, too."

It brought a renewed assurance of His love, but the words that had escaped, "I hate being a woman," shocked me. Where had that feeling been rooted?

I had to draw myself back into my childhood again for an answer.

As a little girl, I had often heard the laments of my paternal grandmother as she looked at me, "It's too bad Sam doesn't have a son." In the Italian culture in which my grandmother was raised, a woman's status was enhanced when she bore male progeny. The subliminal messages I heard was that I had somehow failed my father by being a girl.

As a 10-year-old, I watched the priest at our summer camp say Mass in a cathedral of tall pines, the morning sun glistening through the top branches, while the waves of Lake Huron rolled to the nearby shore. And I could still remember the feeling of sadness that overwhelmed me as I became aware, for the first time, that I would never know God the way he did. A girl could never be a priest.

Had these feelings affected my relationship with God without my knowing it?

I enlarged my search for understanding and reread feminist literature. Authors, such as Gloria Steinem and Marilyn French, wrote about the historical degradation and atrocities perpetrated against women throughout the centuries.

The abuses and discriminations against women had happened to me too.

The feminists and I differed greatly in our viewpoints on abortion, however. Listening to the stories of the women I met and reading literally hundreds of other accounts in books, I found abortion to be the greatest form of exploitation and abuse ever perpetrated against women.

Even my surgically painless abortion was one of the most emotionally painful aspects of my womanhood. It symbolized a complete denial of my uniqueness as a woman. And it showed the depth of my mistrust in God's ability to provide and protect me and my unborn child.

I couldn't help wondering if my hesitancy to abandon myself totally to Jesus wasn't rooted in my perception of my vulnerability as a women.

Gradually sensing His tender compassion over my anger and mistrust, I approached God about the subject of women, one that had haunted me all my life.

"How do you view us, Jesus?" I prayed one night.

"Come walk with me through the Gospels," I heard Him say. So I decided to read straight through, intent on seeing what Jesus' relationship had been with the women around Him.

The dusty roads of Judea, Galilee, Capernium, and Jerusalem were filled with Jesus' followers, both men and women. That fact in itself was unusual: rabbis were not allowed to acknowledge a woman, not even their wives, if they walked by them on the street.

Yet, Jesus consistently was surrounded by women. Many of them are referred to as His friends: Martha and Mary of Bethany, Joanna, Suzanna, and Mary Magdelene. Often, he used women in His illustrations.

My discovery prompted me to dig deeper. The first healing by Jesus recorded at the beginning of His public

life, was that of Simon Peter's mother-in-law. Unlike other rabbis, about whom stories of miraculous healing are recorded, Jesus was the only one who healed women. The truth of that revelation startled me.

The woman with an issue of blood was such a story. Deemed ritually unclean for 12 years, she was made incapable of participation in any community activity. Some traditional writings intimated that her condition made her in some sense displeasing to God. Desperate for healing, she joined the throngs that jostled and pressed around Jesus. Then quietly she reached past tradition and her own fears of reprisal and touched the edge of His cloak. Instantly, her bleeding stopped.

"Who touched me?" Jesus immediately called out.

Dozens of people had touched Him, but He sought the one who needed more than physical healing. For 12 years this woman had been an outcast. Deprived of human touch for so long, her need for acceptance was as great as her need for physical wholeness.

When she stepped forward, she knelt trembling before Him.

"Daughter," He may have said, "you took a risk trusting Me, and now you're healed and whole. Live well, live blessed!"

Jesus' response not only healed her, it helped heal me too. His recognition of her dignity as a woman brought new clarity to my understanding of God's concern for women.

Time and time again, I saw Jesus reaching past the mores of His time and culture to rescue women. One of my favorite stories of concern was of his bringing back to life the widow's dead son:

And when He came near the gate of the city, behold a dead man was being carried out, the only son of his

mother; and she was a widow. And a large crowd from the city was with her. When the Lord saw her, He had compassion on her and said to her, "Do not weep." Then He came and touched the open coffin, and those who carried Him stood still. And He said, "Young man, I say to you, arise." And he who was dead sat up and began to speak. And He presented him to his mother (Luke 7:12-15).

The widow never asked anything of Jesus. His compassion alone compelled Him to restore her son because He understood her need and her grief.

As I continued to pour over the Gospels, I was astounded at how faithful and caring Jesus was to the women around Him, especially in the story of the woman caught in adultery.

Returning from the Mount of Olives, Jesus entered the temple. Suddenly there was a commotion at one end of the courtyard. Long-robed pharisees and religious scholars were dragging a naked woman behind them. They stood her in plain sight, her shame exposed for all to see.

"Teacher," they shouted, "This woman was caught red-handed in the act of adultery. The Law of Moses gives orders to stone such persons. What do you say?"

Jesus bent down and began to write with His finger in the dirt. But they kept hounding Him to give His opinion. Slowly, He straightened up and said, "You who are sinless, throw the first stone." Then He bent down again.

They walked away, one after another, beginning with the oldest.

The woman was left alone with Jesus.

"Woman, where are they? Does no one condemn you?"

"No one, Master."

"Neither do I," said Jesus. "Go on your way. From now

on, don't sin."

These words of acceptance and understanding penetrated deep within my soul. I had done many things in my life that brought inner shame. Often, I felt naked and exposed because of my attitudes and actions. None more painful than my abortion. Knowing the compassion Jesus showed that woman gave me assurance He would do the same for me.

My study in the Gospels freed me from the idea embedded in my soul that my womanhood had been a twist of fate, confining me to a limited involvement in the fullness of life.

Rather, God had a purpose for my life and it was rooted specifically in my womanhood. I began to fall in love with Him in a new way.

Jesus never excluded women from the opportunity to learn of God even though, by Jewish law, women were not allowed to sit under rabbinical teaching. Repeatedly, women surrounded Him as He taught. He even encouraged Mary of Bethany to remain next to Him rather than return to the kitchen to help her sister, Martha. Significantly, He said she chose the better thing to do.

One evening, after reading about His gentle care of women in the Bible, I asked Jesus to allow me to hear from Him personally about women. His answer was the final step toward my acceptance of myself.

"Pat, there are no mistakes in my kingdom. Every individual is wanted and loved by Me. Each has intrinsic value as a reflection of My creation.

"Picture yourself and everyone ever born as a brush stroke on the canvas of my self-portrait. Some are pastel watercolors, dappled gently across the canvas, others are bold, bright oils slapped on with a palette knife, but each brings a new dimension and depth of understanding as to who I am. Therefore, each and every woman is important

to Me; each is a treasure to be cared for and loved for her uniqueness.

"You are one-of-a-kind, unique, and special in every way. There has never been, in all of history, either before or after you, another person just like you."

His words left me embracing my sexuality for the first time with joy. No longer resentful of my womanhood, I was free to forge new avenues with God.

I understood why so many women, deceived and held captive by what they believe to be God's abandonment, would turn away from the One who loved them most, their heavenly Father.

But Jesus came to set the captives free. Women could find new dignity and purpose in their relationship with God, because Jesus was the ultimate liberator.

I began to rejoice in my salvation. I was finally healed, not only from the wounds of my abortion, but from the wounds of self-doubt, of no self-worth. I knew now that I didn't have to work to prove myself worthy. *I was worthy just by being Jesus' child.*

When Mary's friends in Truckee approached me about starting a post-abortion support group for the women in the area, I knew I would see their pain from a new perspective. Now I had my wholeness as a woman of God to share.

One winter morning, five young women sat around a large oak table dappled with bright sunshine. Although all attended the same church, some were not aware that the others had experienced abortions also.

I opened the meeting in prayer, then shared my abortion experience with them. Lindsay, our hostess, spoke next. A tall young woman with a lean, lithe body, she was the epitome of the all-American image.

Beyond the Hidden Pain of Abortion

"The other day I was looking at a picture taken at our wedding hanging in my hallway," she said. "Probably 30 or 35 people are in it, the whole gang we've hung around with for years. And I realized many of the women my age had experienced an abortion. Isn't that amazing?

"I've had two abortions, one when I was 18 and another when I was 21.

"I only got sexually active because I thought that's what I was supposed to do. My friends were having sex with their boyfriends so I thought I should too. My parents never sat down with me to discuss pre-marital sex, so I just assumed it was okay. Stu and I went together for about a year before we starting having sex. I was 17 or 18— yeah I guess I was 18."

As the other women nodded knowingly, Lindsay's hands moved toward her young son lying in a cradle next to her. Carefully she tucked his blanket under his chin.

"When I got pregnant, Stu and I talked about getting married, but we both wanted to go to college. So I had the abortion. He came with me when I had it. Of course, we didn't tell anyone, but we both felt bad. In the fall he went away to college. I stayed home and went to a junior college.

"We broke up for a few years—he went his way, I went mine. When I was 21, I got pregnant again. This time I really struggled. I didn't want to have another abortion. But there was no way I wanted to marry the baby's father. I still loved Stu.

"I called Stu and told him I was pregnant. He felt bad. We even talked again about getting married.

"In the end we decided an abortion was probably the only sensible answer. I was farther along than the first time. After the abortion I started hemorrhaging. They had to do a D & C, then I got an infection. It was a mess. I was sick for months." Her eyes clouded over as she remem-

bered her ordeal.

Two children ran into the kitchen. "Mommy, can we have some cookies?" asked a gravel-voiced four-year-old. His coarse, curly blond hair and pink cheeks mirrored his mother's. She ran her hand through the disheveled mess on the top of his head in an attempt to bring some order to it before she handed him a muffin from the table.

"I've had four abortions." Karen, a lovely, curly haired strawberry blonde with sapphire blue eyes and the Devonshire cream complexion of her Irish ancestry almost whispered her confession.

"I've never had the courage to say that before." She lowered her head and moved her eyes away from us.

"When I first started one-on-one post-abortion counseling with Beth at Lifeline, I couldn't face her with the truth. I only told her about my first abortion. It's still hard for me to believe God can forgive me for what I've done. I know He has, but I mean, how many times can He really forgive the same sin?"

"The apostle Peter asked a similar question, Karen. Do you remember what Jesus answered?" I asked quietly.

Karen nodded affirmatively. "Yes, seventy times seven."

"Do you think Jesus was telling us the truth?"

"Yes, of course," she mumbled as small droplets of tears formed in the corner of her eyes.

"If Jesus asked human beings to offer this kind of forgiveness in His name, doesn't God's unlimited forgiveness cover each and every sin through our entire lives?" I asked.

"Karen, when I prayed about our meeting today, I asked Jesus what He wanted me to tell all of you. I believe His answer was very simple." Slowly I made eye contact with each woman sitting around the table before I finished my sentence.

Beyond the Hidden Pain of Abortion

"'Just tell them I love them.'"

Instantly, tears welled up in each woman's eyes. I knew I'd heard Jesus' voice that morning because they needed to know God had not deserted them, He would always love them, and He had a purpose for their lives.

And I knew that day that I hated the effects of abortion. I saw the same look of pain and disappointment, hurt and self-deprecation cross their faces as I had on so many others I had talked to in the past eight years. Hundreds of miles separated the women in Truckee from those I'd met in Mount Hermon and San Jose, yet the stories were startlingly similar. I was more convinced than ever that abortion was a symptom of a much deeper wound, somehow rooted in each woman's idea of her self-worth.

The spring thaw had begun and it was time to leave Truckee. I left knowing intimacy with Jesus as a child of God was possible. I also knew beyond the shadow of a doubt that God created me and every woman without limitation, a one-of-a-kind expression of His love.

As San Jose loomed ahead on the freeway, I was still thanking Him for the love and support of my family in Truckee and for those who prayed for me during my stay. The writing task God assigned me was completed.

It was January, 1994, Sanctity of Life Sunday. In a few minutes the pastor would call me to the platform to preach the morning message, the first time a woman would fill that role in this congregation. My mission was to bring the healing power of Jesus Christ to those suffering from the pain of abortion.

As I stepped forward and set my Bible on the podium, I looked out at the sea of faces and remembered the night Jesus gathered with His disciples for a final meal together.

He rose from His place, removed His tunic and became a servant. Pouring water into a basin, He knelt down to wash the feet of His treasured friends.

But Simon Peter, appalled by the thought, refused to let Jesus touch him.

Jesus answered Peter, "If I don't wash your feet, you can't be a part of what I'm doing."

I realized many of us were like Peter. We have trouble receiving from the Lord because of what we perceive to be our unworthiness. I had to learn to hold my arms out like the child in the bookstore. He never doubted that his father's open arms would enfold him in safety as he ran into them.

If I had refused Jesus' cleansing, I would have lost the opportunity to gain true intimacy as His follower, as a woman created in His image.

In the past few years I've met vulnerable women of courage throughout the U.S., who have been willing to hand their soiled reputations to Jesus so they could serve others in honesty, speaking the truth in love.

That Sunday I couldn't help wondering what would happen if every woman bound by the pain and grief of abortion stood to speak the truth, to risk her reputation by telling young women what the lifelong consequences were. How many would be saved from the same wounding? If only those women sitting in the church congregations throughout America would stand up in the love of God and speak the truth, how many young women would be spared?

Jesus' words of sacrificial love suddenly flooded my mind, *"Oh Jerusalem, Jerusalem...How often I wanted to gather your children together, as a hen gathers her chicks under her wings, but you were not willing!"* (Matt. 23:37).

How like Jesus to use a child-bearing image—a mother hen—to declare how beloved we are in Him.

INSIGHT QUESTIONS FOR CHAPTER 12

1. Describe your perception of a woman's role in life prior to your abortion experience.

2. What did you think was God's opinion of women prior to your abortion experience?

3. If you attended church as a child, what was the role of women in your church environment? How were women treated by the men in your church?

4. Did you ever think gender limited your ability to know God? Explain your answer.

5. Do you believe your abortion experience will prohibit or limit your service to the Body of Christ? Why or why not?

6. List the things you would like to share with other women about your abortion experience.

Epilogue
...
Karen's Story

Karen's story had such a profound and life-changing impact on me, I wanted to share its promise to women.

You might ask, why Karen's story in particular? What makes hers stand out from other women's abortion stories I've heard through the years? All of them share the same human threads: the pain of loss, of guilt, of low self-worth.

To me, her story epitomized the horror abortion can wreak in a woman's life. Yet, as I talked with this young mother in Truckee during the summer of '94, she exuded a peace and self assurance few people ever experience.

The relationship Karen has developed with Jesus is the type of relationship Madame Guyon described in her book, *Experiencing the Depths of Jesus Christ*. When I first heard her story, I knew Karen had reached a level of self-accep-

tance I had yet to attain. Hearing her retell the horrible events of her life snapped something inside of me. I realized Karen's self-acceptance was rooted in her trust in Jesus.

One afternoon in late January, 1992, over lunch in the only Chinese restaurant in Truckee, Karen shared her story with me.

"I grew up in a small town in New Jersey," she began over a cup of hot green tea. "My first boyfriend and I started being sexually active right around the time my parents' marriage started to fall apart, I guess I was about 15. My dad was a typical Irishman; he liked to stop by the local bar on his way home from work on Friday nights. I remember he started taking me with him when I was five or six years old. We always were able to talk to one another, my dad and me. I loved my dad, I still do."

Karen's eyes had a glint of mischieviousness in them as she let a shy grin slip across her face. "My dad's a real character, a true Irishman, he'd say.

"Mom tolerated his behavior for the sake of us kids, I guess, but his drinking got worse when I was probably 14 or so. He started to stay away from the house more, getting home later and later, and then when he did come home he was drunk most of the time. Finally Mom asked him to leave. Once that happened my world really changed.

"Dad and I had always had a special relationship. I wanted to please him. Once my parents started openly talking about a divorce I felt pretty much alone. They were going through their problems. They didn't have much time for us kids. I hadn't had sex with my boyfriend while my dad was around. I really missed being with my dad, so when he left, I turned to my boyfriend for affection.

"When I found out I was pregnant, we wanted to get married. We really loved each other. But my mom thought

we were too young; I was 16, he was 18.

"I wanted my dad to rescue me, to help me keep my baby, but Dad's drinking was at an all time high. The night I told him I was pregnant, he looked at me like I was a slut and said, 'I never did anything to you. Why did you do this? Don't ever do something like this again.' I felt deserted.

"My mom took me to New York City to have it. I was probably five months along. It was a private hospital, and I was placed in the maternity ward, where the patients were mostly older women. The nurses were nice to me. They sedated me on a Friday evening; I remember they were pretty powerful drugs. Then on Saturday morning they injected the saline solution. They told my mother to leave and to come back on Sunday; it would be all over by then. They kept me heavily sedated all weekend so I don't remember much, except feeling really alone and frightened.

"I didn't want the abortion. I don't remember the baby moving. Maybe I blocked it out of my mind. Before I left the hospital, I remember the nurse telling my mother I'd probably would need counseling when I got home, but my mom never mentioned it again. They gave me pills to dry up my milk and breast pads to take home with me. I was embarrassed—I didn't want my brother and sisters to know what happened.

"My boyfriend had been the only guy I slept with, but after my abortion my dad forbade me to see him. He said, 'If I ever see that guy around here again, or if he tries to see you, he's going to get hurt real bad.' My dad knew some pretty sleazy characters, so my boyfriend stayed away. We never talked or saw each other after that."

"What kind of kid were you before your abortion?" I was interested in knowing if Karen's life had changed like that of so many of the other women I talked with.

"Before my abortion I was a straight kid: above average student, into sports, on the school color guard team.

"My dad bought me a bikini when I got back from New York. I think he wanted to make me feel better. But you know, I think it set me up. I mean, on the one hand he told me never to do anything like that again, then on the other he buys me a bikini so I can show off my body. It was a double message.

"After my abortion I started going to school buzzed. In the morning for breakfast I'd drink a beer and smoke a joint to get ripped. I'd hit school already wasted. My grades dropped. I started cheating a lot, just to pass. My friends stopped hanging out with me; they said I'd gotten too weird.

"Summer came and I really partied down. I started doing drugs: peyote, speed, LSD. My life seemed to just get more and more out of control. Loads of booze, too. That was my drug of choice.

"By that time Dad was totally out of control. One night Mom called the police and had him arrested right in front of the whole neighborhood. Dad moved out for good and Mom's boyfriend moved in. My mom started getting really ticked at me—I knew I'd disappointed her. One night I came home drunk. I guess I reminded her of my dad because she started yelling at me. Then she turned to my brother and sisters who were watching television in the living room and yelled, 'You know what your smart-ass sister did? She went and got pregnant. It cost me $350 to bail her out—now look at her.'

"I was so hurt. Up until that time my little sister had always looked up to me. She took it real hard. 'I can't believe you did that,' she said later. After that I never confided in my mom again. I think she was always jealous of my relationship with my dad.

"My dad lives in New Jersey still. I haven't seen him in

a couple of years." Karen's face reflected a sorrow at the loss of her relationship with her dad now that she lived in California. "I talk to him every once and awhile. He's been sober for a few years now.

"It was during the summer of my abortion that I started getting promiscuous. I'd lost all respect for myself. I'd go to a party, end up in bed with someone, and then I felt compelled to have a relationship with the guy because I'd slept with him.

"I went with guys I wouldn't even have looked at before my abortion. Some of them were really mixed up. I'd bring them home just to piss my mother off.

"When I was 18, I had my second abortion; it was much worse than the first. This time I went to a Planned Parenthood clinic. There we were, about 20 of us in one room, having saline abortions. We weren't given much attention because there were so many women at the clinic.

"I could feel my baby thrashing around, kicking inside my womb. We just lay there having contractions; some of the girls were whimpering, others screaming. The girl next to me couldn't have been more than about 15. She was so frightened. She reminded me of myself when I had my first abortion. I heard her whimpering, so I reached over and held her hand for awhile. We didn't speak to each other. We were on our own.

"For the most part we just lay there and gave birth to dead babies."

Her words slashed across my consciousness. Karen began to cry softly. The horror of the scene she described caught me off guard. It was a form of barbarity I had never imagined. I heard my own soft sobs join hers. The raw brutality of what Karen experienced began to grip me. How many women shared Karen's nightmare? And it was all in the name of freedom.

"After that, my relationships got sleazier and sleazier," Karen continued. "Anytime I did something well, I'd eventually blow it. I'd prove to myself once again I wasn't worthy of success. My life became periods of peaks and valleys. In my early 20's I started doing cocaine. Money was always good; I was a waitress, a bartender, I managed banquets. But I went with one bad guy after another. There seemed to be an out-of-control force in my life. It was as if I had lost my right to say no. And I never used birth control.

"I got married at 24 to Eli. He was a pretty straight guy, an Israeli, but he was in trouble because he didn't have a green card. I liked him so I married him to help him out. My dad came down to the courthouse. I really wanted to make the marriage work, but I wasn't a Jewish princess. We were together for a year. I think we started to fall in love with one another. I know I did.

"He went to Israel to visit his family. While he was gone I found out I was pregnant. I told everyone, I was so excited. I could finally have the baby I'd always wanted.

"When he returned from Israel, he wasn't excited about the baby at all. His aunt said she would take me to upstate New York to see her doctor: 'You should get a check-up,' she said. 'You should meet my doctor, he's wonderful.'

"After examining me the doctor said I was still in my first trimester, so he could do it right there in the office. Once I realized what he was talking about I got up and ran out into the parking lot. I didn't want them to take my baby from me. Eli and his aunt ran outside after me. I was so hurt. I thought Eli loved me, and in a way I know he did, but it was obvious he wanted his children to be Jewish. I was just a *shiksa*, a blond, blue eyed American girl who helped him get his green card. He didn't want me to be the mother of his children." Karen stopped and looked away a moment. Then she looked down and shook

her head in disbelief. "It seems like a nightmare to me now; my life has changed so much since then."

"Do you want to stop? We don't have to continue if you don't want to," I said.

"No, no, I want to go on. In a way it's good to tell it all in one setting; it's like a cleansing. Anyway, after I ran to the parking lot, I realized I couldn't go anywhere. His aunt persuaded me to come back in. I didn't feel I could stop it.

"The doctor didn't give me any medication. He said he couldn't give me anything because his office wasn't considered a clinic, or something like that, I don't really remember exactly what he said. I just remember he had me lie down on the examining table, and he turned on the suction machine and started scraping. Eli's aunt stayed with me and held my hand, but the pain wasn't that bad. I cried, but not because of the physical pain. I cried because they took my baby away from me.

"Eli left me with his aunt for a few days. I wanted to go home with him. I needed him to be there for me, but they thought I should stay with her. She had three small children. Being with them, watching them play, and hug their mom and dad, made me sad. I always loved kids, and I wanted my baby back.

"Once I returned to New Jersey my relationship with Eli fell apart. My life went downhill after that. I got pregnant again. Had another abortion. When I went for my last abortion, I lied and told them I'd only had one, one other time, I didn't tell them it was my fourth. You know, all those times, no one ever told me of the potential risks or dangers I might face. I was never given counseling either before or after any of them. After my last abortion I just drove myself home."

Karen lowered her head and played with the spoon lying next to her cup. Her story epitomized the stories I

209

had heard over and over again. During her parents' divorce Karen had floundered without the affection and affirmation her father always provided.

Eventually, the turmoil associated with their divorce made her vulnerable and needy. Emotionally abandoned by them, she turned to her boyfriend for the affection her father was no longer able to give her. Too young to fully comprehend the physical and emotional consequences her sexual involvement might bring, she was unprepared for her pregnancy.

Although Karen wanted to keep her baby, her parents, caught in the turmoil of their own lives, were unwilling to help her accept responsibility for her child. Because she had wanted her baby, her abortion triggered a form of self-hatred. She linked her gradual spiral down into a life of self-abasement directly to the lack of self-worth she felt after her first abortion.

Like so many of the women I met, Karen had endured a great deal of physical, psychological, and emotional abuse due to her need for love and reassurance.

I lowered my eyes trying to hide my tears. In the months I had known Karen I had grown to love her as a daughter. She had managed to pull herself out of her tailspin and had established a healthy and successful relationship with her husband and child.

"Karen, I'm fascinated by what you've been able to do with your life after so much abuse and pain. What happened to you? Your life today is so different from the one you just described."

"My husband Chris was the first person I loved more than alcohol. He had a lot to do with me getting off the emotional roller coaster I was on.

But my life really began to change when I dedicated my life to Jesus. It was coming to understand and then believe

210

God loved me, no matter what I had done in my past, that caused me to begin to forgive myself. He's the real hero in my life."

I could see that what Karen said was true. Her sense of self-worth, after all that she had been through, was phenomenal to me. And it was anchored, she assured me, in her understanding of Jesus' love for her. It was apparent that Karen had come to a point of acceptance about herself and her abortions that would point the way to the rest of us.

I thought again of Madame Guyon's words of invitation. Through her words, Jesus was inviting us to enter into a life of purpose and peace with Him:

I give you an invitation: If you are thirsty, come to the living waters. Do not waste your precious time digging wells that have no water in them.

If you are starving and can find nothing to satisfy your hunger, then come. Come, and you will be filled.

You who are poor, come.

You who are afflicted, come.

You who are weighted down with your load of wretchedness and your load of pain, come. You will be comforted.[1]

Perhaps you are like Karen. Your life has been out of control, filled with self depreciation and a lack of self-worth.

Jesus wants to bring a new life to you today, filled with hope and an abundance of God's love. If you want to develop a relationship with Jesus like Karen's, simply turn your life back to God and pray this simple prayer:

Beyond the Hidden Pain of Abortion

Heavenly Father,

If I look at my life, it seems too shattered to be put back together again. I know I can't go any further alone. You healed Karen. And now, Lord, I ask You to heal me, too. Thank you, Father for being willing to do that for me.

I don't know how I strayed so far from You. Lead me back home to You and to life everlasting.

I thank you for faithfully waiting for me. Don't let me escape out of your arms again. Hold me close to You always.

Thank you for giving your Son, Jesus, so that in His death, I can find life and be whole again. Thank you, heavenly Father for loving me. Show me Your way.

Amen.

Source Notes

CHAPTER FOUR

1. Catherine Marshall, *A Man Called Peter* (New York: Fawcett World Library, 1951), p. 39.
2. Ibid., p. 176.
3. Ibid., p. 178.
4. Ibid.
5. Ibid.
6. Ibid.

CHAPTER SEVEN

1. Carole Gift Page, *Misty, Our Momentary Child*

(Westchester, IL: Crossway, 1987), p. 49.
2. Ibid., p. 58.
3. Ibid., p. 60.
4. Ibid., p. 63.
5. Ibid., p. 103.
6. Ibid., p. 104.

CHAPTER ELEVEN

1. Jeanne Guyon, *Experiencing the Depths of Jesus Christ* (Maine: Christian Books, 1975). p. ix.
2. Ibid., p. 2.
3. Ibid., p. 1.
4. Ibid., p. 1.

EPILOGUE

1. Jeanne Guyon, *Experiencing the Depths of Jesus Christ* , p. 2.

Support Groups–
Places of Growth
and Healing

Women are hungry for teaching and nurturing as they grapple with issues that touch them where they live—loss, self-worth, singleness, remarriage, and numerous other felt needs.

God's heart is to heal and restore his people. In fact, Jesus states this clearly in Luke 4:18, 19 when he announces that God has called him to minister to the oppressed, the hurting, and the brokenhearted. We read throughout the entire New Testament how he wants to equip the Body of Christ to join him in reaching out in love and support of the bruised and wounded. Support groups provide this special place where healing can happen—where women are given time and space to be open about themselves in the context of loving acceptance and honest caring.

WHAT IS A SUPPORT GROUP?

• A support group is a small-group setting which offers women a "safe place." The recommended size is from eight to ten people.

• It is a compassionate, nonthreatening, confidential place where women can be open about their struggles and receive caring and support in a biblically-based, Christ-centered atmosphere.

• It is an accepting place, where women are listened to and loved right where they are.

• It is a place where love and truth are shared and the Holy Spirit is present to bring God's healing.

• It is a place where women learn to take responsibility for making Christ-like choices in their own lives.

• A support group has designated leadership. Co-leaders are strongly recommended to share the role of facilitators.

• It is a cohesive and consistent group. This implies "closing" it to additional participants after the second or third meeting before beginning with a new topic.

WHAT SUPPORT GROUPS ARE NOT

• They are not counseling groups.

• They are not places to "fix" or change women.

• They are not Bible study or prayer groups as such, although Scripture and prayer are a natural framework for the meetings.

• They are not places where women concentrate on themselves and "stay there." Instead they provide opportunity to grow in self-responsibility and wholeness in Christ.

Small groups often rotate leadership among participants, but because support groups usually meet for a specific time period with a specific mutual issue, it works

well for a team of co-leaders to be responsible for the meetings. As you can see, leadership is important! Let's take a look at it.

WHAT ARE THE PERSONAL LEADERSHIP QUALIFICATIONS OF A SUPPORT GROUP LEADER?

Courage (1 Cor. 16:13, 14)

A leader shows courage in the following ways in her willingness to:

• Be open to self-disclosure, admitting her own mistakes and taking the same risks she expects others to take.

• Lovingly explore areas of struggle with women, and look beyond their behavior to hear what's in their hearts.

• Be secure in her own beliefs, sensitive to the Holy Spirit's promptings, and willing to act upon them.

• Draw on her own experiences to help her identify with others in the group and be emotionally touched by them.

• Consistently examine her own life in the light of God's Word and the Holy Spirit's promptings.

• Be direct and honest with members, not use her role to protect herself from interaction with the group.

• Know that wholeness is the goal and that change is a process.

Willingness to Model (Ps. 139:23, 24)

• A group leader should have had moderate victory in her own struggles, with adequate healing having taken place. If she is not whole in the area she is leading, she should at least be fully aware of her unhealed areas and not be defensive of them. She should be open to those who can show her if she is misguiding others by ministering out of her own hurt.

217

• She understands that group leaders lead largely by example, by doing what she expects members to do.

• She is no longer "at war" with her past and can be compassionate to those who may have victimized her. Yet she is a "warrior woman," strong in her resistance of Satan with a desire to see other captives set free.

Presence (Gal. 6:2)

• A group leader needs to either have had personal experience with a support group or observed enough so she understands how they function.

• A group leader needs to be emotionally present with the group members, being touched by others' pain, struggles, and joys.

• She needs to be in touch with her own feelings so that she can have compassion for and empathy with the other women.

• She must understand that her role is as a facilitator. She is not to be the answer person nor is she responsible for change in others. Yet she must be able to evidence leadership qualities that enable her to gather a group around her.

Goodwill and Caring (Matt. 22:27, 28)

• A group leader needs to express genuine caring, even for those who are not easy to care for. That takes a commitment to love and a sensitivity to the Holy Spirit.

• She should be able to express caring by (1) inviting women to participate but allowing them to decide how far to go; (2) giving warmth, concern, and support when, and only when, it is genuinely felt; (3) gently confronting a participant when there are obvious discrepancies between her words and her behavior; and (4) encouraging people to be who they are without their masks and shields.

• She will need to be able to maintain focus in the group.

Openness (Eph. 4:15, 16)

• A group leader must be aware of herself, open to others in the group, open to new experiences, and open to life-styles and values that are different from her own.

• As the leader she needs to have an *attitude* of openness, not revealing every aspect of her personal life, but disclosing enough of herself to give participants a sense of who she is.

• A group leader needs to recognize her own weaknesses and not spend energy concealing them from others. A strong sense of awareness allows her to be vulnerable with the group.

Nondefensiveness (1 Pet. 5:5)

• A group leader needs to be secure in her leadership role. When negative feelings are expressed she must be able to explore them in a nondefensive manner.

Stamina (Eph. 6:10)

• A group leader needs physical and emotional stamina and the ability to withstand pressure and remain vitalized until the group sessions end.

• She must be aware of her own energy level, have outside sources of spiritual and emotional nourishment, and have realistic expectations for the group's progress.

Perspective (Prov. 3:5, 6)

• A group leader needs to cultivate a healthy perspective which allows her to enjoy humor and be comfortable with the release of it at appropriate times in a meeting.

• Although she will hear pain and suffering, she must trust the Lord to do the work and not take responsibility for what he alone can do.

• She needs to have a good sense of our human condition

and God's love, as well as a good sense of timing that allows her to trust the Holy Spirit to work in the women's lives.

Creativity (Phil. 1:9-11)

• She needs to be flexible and spontaneous, able to discover fresh ways to approach each session.

WHAT SPECIFIC SKILLS DOES A LEADER NEED?

A support group leader needs to be competent and comfortable with basic group communications skills. The following five are essential for healthy and open interaction:

Rephrase

• Paraphrase back to the speaker what you thought she said. Example: "I hear you saying that you felt. . . ."

Clarify

• To make sure you heard correctly ask the speaker to explain further. Example: "I'm not hearing exactly what you meant when you said. . . ."

Extend

• Encourage the speaker to be more specific. Example: "Can you give us an example. . . ."

Ask for Input

• Give the other women opportunity to share their opinions. Example: "Does anyone else have any insight on this?"

Be Personal and Specific

• Use women's names and convey "I" messages instead of "you" messages. "I'm feeling afraid of your reaction, " instead of "You scare me."

ADDITIONAL COMMUNICATION SKILLS

Active Listening

• A good listener learns to "hear" more than the words that are spoken. She absorbs the content, notes the gestures, the body language, the subtle changes in voice or expression, and senses the unspoken underlying messages.

• As a good listener, a leader will need to discern those in the group who need professional counseling and be willing to address this.

Empathy

• This requires sensing the subjective world of the participant—and caring. Of grasping another's experience and at the same time listening objectively.

Respect and Positive Regard

• In giving support, leaders need to draw on the positive assets of the members. Where differences occur, there needs to be open and honest appreciation and acceptance.

• Leaders must be able to maintain confidentiality and instill that emphasis in the group.

Expressing Warmth

• Smiling is especially important in communicating warmth to a group. Other nonverbal expressions are voice tone, posture, body language, and facial expression.

Genuineness

• Leaders need to be real, to be themselves in relating with others, to be authentic and spontaneous, to realize that the Holy Spirit works naturally.

WHAT DOES A LEADER ACTUALLY DO?

The leader will need to establish the atmosphere of the support group and show by her style how to relate lovingly and helpfully in the group. She needs to have God's heart for God's people. The following outline specific tasks.

She organizes logistics

• The leader helps arrange initial details of the early meetings—time, place, books, etc. (Note: Leaders need to be aware that much secular material, though good in information, is humanistic in application. "I" and "Self" are the primary focus, rather than Christ.)

She provides sense of purpose and vision

• She reminds the group of their purpose from time to time so that the group remains focused.

She acts as the initiator

• She makes sure everyone knows each other, helps them get acquainted and feel comfortable with each other. Makes sure meetings start and end on time.

She continues as an encourager to group members

• This basically means encouraging feelings to be expressed, keeping the atmosphere nonjudgmental and accepting, giving feedback, answering questions, clarifying things that were expressed, etc. Praying with and for members.

She sets expectations

• She models openness and interest in the group. She must be willing to take risks by resolving conflicts and clarifying intentions. She holds up standards of confiden-

tiality personally and by reminding the group at each meeting. Confidentiality is crucial to the health of a group, and women should not divulge any private sharing, even to spouses, family, etc.

• She must be watchful and able to guide individuals away from destructive responses. Example: "I have a right to be hurt." She will need to always separate the person from her behavior, meeting the person where she is. Example: "We accept that you are hurt. Do you need to talk about it?"

She is sensitive to the Spirit

• She must know when someone needs to be referred to a professional counselor, pastor, etc., and be willing to work that problem through.

• She should be comfortable in ministering freely in the gifts of the Holy Spirit.

She gives the guidelines

• It is important that the women know the "ground rules." The leader needs to repeat these often, and *always* when newcomers attend. The following are basic support group guidelines:

1. You have come to give and receive support. No "fixing." We are to listen, support, and be supported by one another, not give advice.

2. Let other members talk. Please let them finish without interruption.

3. Try to step over any fear of sharing in the group. Yet do not monopolize the group's time.

4. Be interested in what someone else shares. Listen with your heart. Never converse privately with someone while another woman is talking or belittle her beliefs or expressions.

5. Be committed to express your feelings from the heart. Encourage others to do the same. It's all right to feel angry, to laugh, or to cry.

6. Help others own their feelings and take responsibility for change in their lives. Don't jump in with an easy answer or a story on how you conquered their problem or automatically give scripture as a "pat answer." Relate to where they are.

7. Avoid accusing or blaming. Speak in the "I" mode about how something or someone made you feel. Example: "I felt angry when. . . ."

8. Avoid ill-timed humor to lighten emotionally charged times. Let participants work through their sharing even if it is hard.

9. Keep names and sharing of other group members confidential.

10. Because we are all in various stages of growth, please give others permission to be where they are in their growth. This is a "safe place" for all to grow and share their lives.

She handles group discussion

Everyone is different. Your support group will have a variety of personalities. As a leader you will need to protect the group from problem behavior and help the individuals work through it. The following are examples of ways to help each person contribute so that the group benefits:

THEIR BEHAVIOR	YOUR ACTION
Too talkative	Interject by summarizing what the talker is saying. Turn to someone else in the group and redirect a question: "Elaine, what do you feel about that?"

A "fixer"	Show appreciation for their help and insight. Then direct a question to someone else. It is important to draw others in so that the woman needing help gets a healthy perspective on her situation and doesn't close off with a quickie solution.
Rambler	Thank them. If necessary, even break in, comment briefly, and move the discussion on.
Antagonist	Recognize legitimate objections when you can. Turn their comments to a constructive view. If all else fails, discuss the attitude privately and ask for their help.
Obstinate	Ask them to clarify. They may honestly not understand what you're talking about. Enlist others to help them see the point. If that doesn't work, tell them you will discuss the matter after the meeting.
Wrong topic	Focus on the subject. Say something such as: "Mary, that's interesting, but tonight we're talking about. . . ."
Her own problems	Bring it into the discussion if it is related. Otherwise, acknowledge

225

	the problem and say: "Yes, I can see why that hurts you. Could we talk about it privately?"
Controversial questions	State clearly what you can or cannot discuss. Say something such as: "Problems do exist, but we do not discuss political issues here."
Side conversations	Stop and draw them into your discussion by asking for their ideas.
Personality clash	If a dispute erupts, cut across with a direct question on the topic. Bring others into the discussion: "Let's concentrate on the issue and not make this a personal thing."
Wrong choice of words	Point out that their idea is good and then help them by putting their idea into your words. Protect them from ridicule.
Definitely wrong	Make a clear comment, in an affirming way. "That's another point of view and of course you're entitled to your opinion." Then move on.
Bored	Try to find where their area of interest is. Draw them in to share their experience.

Question you can't answer	Redirect the question to the group. If you don't know the answer, say so and offer to find out.
Never participates	Use direct questions. Remind the group that they will get more out of the meeting when they open up.
Quiet, unsure of self	Affirm them in the eyes of the group. Ask direct questions you are sure they can answer.

She evaluates the meeting

• Support groups are a growing experience for everyone, including the leader. Don't be afraid to deal with habitual problems.

• Periodically involve the total group in evaluating how things are going.

She understands conflict and can handle it positively

• She understands the biblical pattern for making peace with our sisters in Christ. (See Matthew 5:9 and Romans 14:19.)

• She understands that Jesus has given us clear guidelines to resolve conflict and effect reconciliation and that our motive must be to demonstrate God's love, not vengeance. (See Matthew 5:23, 24 and Matthew 18:15-17.)

• She understands that we approach all situations humbly, knowing that none of us is without sin (Gal. 6:1-4) and that we are seeking reconciliation and forgiveness, not proving who is right and who is wrong.

• She avoids sermonizing.

• She knows that every group will experience conflict

on their way to becoming mature and effective, but uses it to help clarify goals and boundaries for the group.

• She defines and describes the conflict as "our group problem."

• She deals with issues rather than personalities.

• She takes one issue at a time.

• She tries to catch issues while they are small rather than letting them escalate over time.

• She invites cooperation, rather than intimidating or giving ultimatums.

• She expresses need for full disclosure of all the facts rather than allowing hidden agendas or leftover hurt feelings.

• She tries to maintain a friendly, trusting attitude.

• She recognizes others' feelings and concerns and opts for a "win-win" feeling rather than an "us and them" attitude.

• She encourages the expression of as many new ideas and as much new information as possible to broaden the perspective of all involved.

• She involves every woman in the conflict at a common meeting.

• She clarifies whether she is dealing with one conflict or several on-going ones.

She knows how to use feedback

• Feedback helps another person get information on her behavior.

• Feedback is essential in a support group to help the women keep on target and more effectively move through her problems.

• She helps make feedback specific. Example: "Just now when we were talking about forgiveness, you changed the subject and started to blame your brother."

• She directs feedback toward behavior that the receiver can do something about. Example: "Would you like to make a choice to release your judgment against your friend?"

• She takes into account the needs of both the receiver and the giver of feedback. It can be destructive if it's given to "straighten out" someone, rather than lovingly point out where that person is.

• She knows feedback is most useful when it is asked for. She can say: "Margaret, are you open to some feedback?"

• She watches for good timing. She tries to give feedback at the earliest opportunity after the given behavior occurs.

• She checks to ensure clear communication. One way of doing this is to have the receiver paraphrase the feedback to see if that is what the sender meant. Example: "I heard you saying that I need to examine my motives for. . . ."

ONE FINAL WORD

Be encouraged if the Lord has called you to be a support group leader or a member of a group. The Lord promises to do the work of healing, to be with us, to grant us patience, love, mercy—everything we need to follow his commission to love. There will be hard and even painful times. But we can count on him. "He who began a good work in you (in us) will carry it on to completion until the day of Christ Jesus" (Phil. 1:6).

A Special Note
to Prospective Aglow Support Group Leaders

In January, 1994, Aglow introduced a new opportunity for existing and prospective Aglow support group leaders. With the publication of our own *Support Group Leader's Guide* by Jennie Newbrough, (Aglow, 1993), came the chance to standardize our training material and award a Certificate of Completion to women who read our leader's guide and successfully complete the worksheets at the back of the book.

Because support group leaders touch some of the most intimate areas of women's lives, new Aglow support group leaders must possess a Certificate of Completion awarded by the Aglow leadership before they can begin leading a group. Those who receive Aglow's Certificate of Completion also must understand that doing so only allows them to lead an Aglow support group within the Aglow ministry.

Jennie Newbrough, Aglow's support group resource person, believes God has been powerfully using these compassionate "safe places" to transform the lives of countless women. If you feel that God is speaking to you about leading a support group around the topic in this book, we urge you to make your desire known to local Aglow leadership. Let's join in sharing Father God's heart for hurting women.

BOOKS BY AGLOW PUBLICATIONS
Heart Issues

Marilyn Fanning   **Compassionate Care**
Practical Love for Your Aging
Parents

Heather Harpham   **Daddy, Where Were You?**
Healing for the Father-deprived
Daughter

General Books

Jane Hansen with   **Inside a Women**
Carol Greenwood   Revealing Her Longings, Pain,
and the Journey to Love

Jane Hansen and   **Women of Prayer**
other Aglow leaders   Released to the Nations

Jennie Newbrough   **Support Group Leader's Guide**

Quin Sherrer   **How to Pray for Your Children**

Bible Studies

Basic Series

God's Daughter
Practical Aspects of a Christian Woman's Life

The Holy Spirit and His Gifts
A Study of the Scriptural Gifts

Coming Alive in the Spirit
The Spirit-Led Life

Discovering the Heart of God Series

Called to Spiritual Maturity
A Study of Hebrews, Chapters 1-4

Getting to Know the Heart of God
A Study of Hebrews, Chapters 5-10

Practicing Truth in the Family of God
A Study of Hebrews, Chapters 11-13

We at Aglow encourage you to order toll free at 1-800-755-2456, or order from your local Christian bookstore. Write for a free catalog:

> Communications Dept.
> Aglow
> P.O. Box 1548
> Lynnwood, WA 98046-1548
> USA
> FAX (206) 778-9615

Inquiries regarding speaking availability and other correspondence may be directed to Pat Bigliardi at the following address:

Patricia A. Bigliardi
Face to Face Ministries
1685 Branham Lane #105
San Jose, CA 95118
USA

FAX # 408-266-3289
1-800-Pattie B